Contents

List of tables and figures

Acknowledgements

This work would not have been possible
without the willing and supportive co-operation
of those running, volunteering in, using, or
otherwise involved with local food projects
around the country. We are extremely grateful to
all who gave up their time to share their
experience, ideas and insights with us. We have
tried to do justice to their work in this report.

Our warmest thanks also go to members of
the Foundation's Advisory Group, who gave us
excellent, timely guidance, and to our funders,
the Joseph Rowntree Foundation; in particular,
Barbara Ballard, who supported and steered our
work with great insight and care.

1 Introduction

Our new Government was elected on a ... pledge to ... tackle the root causes of illness. We are committed to reducing inequalities in health, ... to attack[ing] the underlying causes of ill-health and to break[ing] the cycle of social and economic deprivation and social exclusion.

(Tessa Jowell, Minister for Public Health, July 1997)

There is a new public agenda for addressing inequality: regenerating local communities, improving health, and redressing the consequences of increasing poverty and deprivation. Government policy calls for partnership between public, voluntary and private sectors to work together with those who live on low incomes and in deprivation to enable them to achieve a better quality of life. There is an interest in process: how to improve and co-ordinate decision making and negotiation to develop practical solutions to tangible problems.

The policy context

In 1996, the Low Income Project Team to the Nutrition Task Force of *Health of the Nation* published its report on examples of good local practice which enable those who live on low incomes to eat a healthier diet. The report called for the establishment of a database on, and network between, local projects as part of a national strategy for food and low income. Partnerships between the local community, the public and private sectors, particularly food retailers, were promoted as a way forward for strengthening local activities. Little evidence of a national, co-ordinated approach to food problems for those who live on low incomes emerged in the subsequent months, but there was continuing enthusiasm for local food projects and initiatives. However, the Low Income Project Team report had highlighted that local projects, while important in their own terms in enabling some people to gain access to an adequate variety of good quality, affordable food, could not provide comprehensive coverage and integrated solutions at regional and national levels. They lacked funds for long-term development, were often isolated in activity, and relied heavily on volunteers. Food activities for the poor were confined to the periphery of regenerative proposals.

In February 1998, the Green Paper, *Our Healthier Nation: A Contract for Health*, was published (Department of Health, 1998). This publication was the first from Government to acknowledge that poverty and deprivation are prime causes of ill health and mortality, and that improving the health of the worst off in society was a principal aim. Access to food was one of the key factors listed as contributing to health inequalities, along with the lack of opportunity that people on low incomes have to put their knowledge about what is good for health into practice. The Green Paper also recognised shared responsibilities for action. It referred to a contract or partnership between public, voluntary and private sectors at national, local, community and individual levels.

This Green Paper drew on the considerable evidence, published over the previous five years and more, which identified major contributors to inequalities in health (Hills, 1995; Wilkinson, 1996; Gordon and Patanzis, 1997; Acheson, 1998), key amongst which is food (Department of Health, 1994; Leather, 1996; James *et al.*, 1997).

Earlier policy recommendations to address the food problems of low income households and communities (Benzeval *et al.*, 1995; Department of Health, 1996) are now strengthened by more fundamental and widespread approaches (Acheson, 1998; National Food Alliance, 1998). Local or community food projects still feature in the recommendations, but the agenda has widened: partnerships, long-term commitment to community development and integrated national government policy are features of the new approach to public health.

This was developed further with the publication in September 1998 of the Social Exclusion Unit Report: *Bringing Britain Together: A National Strategy for Neighbourhood Renewal* (Social Exclusion Unit, 1998). In it, a national strategy to reduce the gap between the poorest neighbourhoods and the rest of the country was set out. Its critical aims are to invest in people, rather than buildings; to involve communities in planning and managing decisions, and to build skills and neighbourhood institutions, rather than parachuting in professionals with short-term solutions; and to sustain long-term political commitment to integrated policies. It seeks lessons from good practice at the local level. Eighteen cross-cutting Action Teams are being created as a fast-track contribution to the policy-making process. Three are particularly pertinent to food: Community Self-help (No. 9: to encourage and strengthen volunteering); 'Schools Plus' (No. 11: to support homework centres, breakfast clubs and summer schools); and Shops (No. 13: to identify best practice and innovative approaches to improving poor neighbourhoods' access to food and services).

This document is important because it signifies a change in the policy context, from an exclusive demand for value for money hard outcomes, delivered in the short term, to a recognition that sustainability and participation, shared ownership and capacity building are key to reducing inequalities and deprivation. There is an interest in 'what works': what enables initiatives to get off the ground, to become sustainable, to adapt and move on, and what are the appropriate ways to measure effectiveness and sustainability. This research was set up to address those questions in relation to local food projects.

Local food projects

What are 'local food projects'? There is no formal definition, but they broadly encompass a range of initiatives which operate in a given community, or which have arisen from a local group within a community (Anderson *et al.*, 1996). The label is usually attached to projects which work with, or are generated by, low income communities. Sometimes the activity could be seen as an extension to a professional's job; sometimes it is something quite new for an area. Some activities are stand-alone; some are part of larger projects or ventures. They operate under a variety of sectors: in some instances, as part of community development initiatives; in others, under the aegis of promoting and improving public health. All have some connection with food: supply, quality, range of commodities, skills or experience, taste or consumption.

The Health Education Board in Scotland recently funded a review of the range and work of Scottish community food projects which aimed to overcome one or more of the barriers generally perceived to prevent people from obtaining an adequate, healthy diet (Anderson *et al.*, 1996). In England and Wales, the Nutrition Task Force to *Health of the Nation* acknowledged that 'people on limited incomes may experience particular difficulties in obtaining a healthy and varied diet', and that 'the most effective way to assist people on low incomes … is by encouraging effective local intiatives and projects' (Department of Health, 1994, p. 32). Substantial efforts have been made by the National Food Alliance (NFA), the Health Education Authority (HEA), The Poverty Alliance and the Scottish Community Diet Project to publicise the diversity of projects, foster communication and exchange of skills between projects, and to support their development (National Food Alliance, 1994, 1995–98; National Food Alliance/Health Education Authority, 1996; Killeen, 1997; The Poverty Alliance Foodworks Team, 1997; Scottish Community Diet Project, 1998).

One could reasonably ask, are local food projects any different from other community, voluntary sector initiatives, such as fitness or exercise clubs; self-help groups to combat addictive behaviours such as smoking, alcohol or drugs; or credit unions, clothing exchanges or advice centres? There are clear similarities: all (except perhaps clothing exchanges) are oriented to personal change and achievement; many address structural and access problems faced by low income households; many rely on volunteers to maintain and energise them. There are also important differences: 'food' is a more complicated issue, for individuals, households and communities, than, say, credit or clothes. Food choice and management are a daily habit, yet also part of self and family identity, deeply embedded in cultural, social and religious beliefs and practice. Food is private, in that it is stored and consumed in the domestic domain; yet it is also communal (shopping, eating) and therefore a public good, because few grow or rear their own food. Access to food – that is, the shops or markets people can reach, what they can buy and for how much – is governed by decisions and practice in which few ordinary citizens play any part. Initiatives to change factors within the complex business of obtaining, preparing and consuming food are bound to be varied in nature and outcome. Local food projects are clearly seen in different ways by different people investing in that process. For these reasons, local food projects are difficult to define and understanding how they work is not a straightforward matter. Yet it is important to do so to appreciate what they contribute and what facilitates their sustainability.

Local food projects and why they work

The primary aims of this project were to select a cross-section of different types of local or community food projects, spanning a wide geographical spread, in order to:

- investigate the factors which lead to the establishment and sustainability of local food initiatives, particularly those which address the needs of identified low income groups

- determine the extent to which the initial project aims, especially process aims, have been achieved

- understand the social context in which such projects become established.

The methods used to contact and investigate the local food projects are described in the next chapter. Essentially, some 25 initiatives were investigated, spanning a wide range of activities. Document analysis, in-depth interviews and focus groups were used to examine what facilitated or hindered projects from 'working', from being sustainable, in order to draw on the experience of those who had been involved. We did not set out to evaluate the projects, nor to describe their workings in detail. We do not identify them in this report, or even where they are. We all found the research rewarding and satisfying, because we met such amazing people and heard such astonishing stories of initiative, vision and hard work. Projects were very welcoming (none of those we approached refused to take part). They gave us a great deal of time and help, and the people involved, whether as 'users', volunteers or professionals, were all keen to be interviewed and to tell us their story. The people we encountered often said how much they valued the opportunity for reflection which the interview process had afforded them.

We interviewed more than 130 people and ran over 20 focus groups. This produced a complex data set, partly because 'food projects' mean different things to different people: they are a disparate set of activities, and disentangling different perspectives and connections between factors and outcomes took some time. In some projects, it was hard to establish even the basic history, because people and activities had changed so much and so often. In others, the story seemed straightforward, but an interview with someone seemingly peripheral might throw quite a different light. Despite these challenges, the data collected provided us with important insights into how food projects operate.

We have been able to identify a number of broad themes which are examined in the report:

- why projects are set up, including the factors responsible for their initiation

- steps leading to establishment, including funding issues

- the roles played by initiators, leaders, managers, volunteers and users, in sustaining a project in its first phases

- the nature of project outcomes and measures of success, as seen by those involved

- the factors which lead to, or preclude, sustainability, only some of which are related to funding.

The final section of this report examines policy options concerning the development, desirability and sustainability of community food initiatives.

Local people and organisations can easily identify the problems they face and propose solutions. Very often, these solutions cannot be implemented because of the inflexibility of centrally devised programmes and policies. The main obstacles to effective co-ordination at a local level are narrowly defined value for money and other performance indicators; rigid administration so that local actors are not empowered to vire expenditure between sub programmes or area; inflexibility in the face of changing needs.
(National Housing Federation, quoted in the Social Exclusion Unit Report, 1998)

2 Selection of projects, research design and methods

Choice of projects

The Health Education Authority (HEA) and the National Food Alliance (NFA) hold a database of food and low income projects (National Food Alliance/Health Education Authority, 1996). This database proved an essential initial source of information in trying to identify food projects to participate in this research. The database has details of over 120 projects from around the country and it was possible to search on the following criteria: location, usage, project type, management, target audience, user involvement, evaluation and funding.

A total of 18 projects were identified from the HEA/NFA database and a further seven projects were recruited via a range of different methods. In total, the projects chosen reflected a variety of types, with a good geographical spread over England and three projects from Scotland and Wales. Three were primarily rural-based, four were in towns, eight were on the urban fringe and ten were located in inner city areas.

The processes by which the projects were contacted are set out in Appendix 1. The projects were visited by two researchers for a maximum of two days so as to minimise disruption and for ease of organisation, as this meant that, where necessary, more than one interview could be conducted simultaneously.

Projects included in the research

Projects were allocated to one of eight different types, summarised in Table 1. Some project categories were easily identifiable; labels for the others were created by the authors, i.e. nutrition education, combined, food provision and

partnerships. Those projects in transition were categorised according to their recent activity. Further details on the projects are in Appendix 2, along with Carstairs deprivation scores (Carstairs and Morris, 1989) for the area. Project location is not given in the report and projects are not identified because each was guaranteed anonymity.

Research design

Both qualitative and quantitative methods were used to collect data from 25 food projects located throughout the UK. This pluralistic approach was necessary given the wide range of projects and respondents who participated in the study. The methods consisted of semi-structured interviews, telephone interviews, focus groups, self-completion questionnaires and an analysis of files and literature held by the projects. More detail on the methodologies is given in Appendix 3.

Data collection occurred in four stages.

1　Food projects were contacted and preliminary information on the type of project, duration and the number of users was collected.

2　Semi-structured interviews were conducted with those involved in setting up and running the projects. These included both paid staff and volunteers.

3　Focus groups were conducted with users of the food projects. Self-completion questionnaires were used to collect socio-demographic and other information from these respondents.

Table 1 Description of projects

Type of project	Number	Description
Cook & eat	4	The cook & eat sessions ran on a weekly basis, usually for a set number of weeks. Health visitors, dietitians and development workers were involved.
Food co-op	5	The food co-ops were similar to each other, and were held once a week. They usually sold fruit and vegetables. They involved people placing weekly orders which were then collated and packed by volunteers.
Cafés	3	Two of the cafés had church links and were in buildings where other services were on offer, including advice, family support, clothes. The third café was located in a leisure centre, and was run by a paid worker who had been a volunteer in an earlier food-based activity.
Food provision	3	The food provision projects were probably the most diverse. They included a food growing project, run by a professional; a breakfast club, run by a school's catering staff; and a project providing free cooked meals to people in the evenings, run by a professional and by volunteers (with a paid co-ordinator).
Nutrition education	2	These were run by professionals (dietitians). One involved two paid workers (not professionally trained) working under the supervision of a dietetic department. The other involved a dietitian who gave opportunistic nutritional advice in an antenatal clinic, ran a postnatal support group and is developing a tool for collecting dietary information.
Combined	3	These were projects which included more than one type of activity. One included a community centre-based fruit and vegetable shop, promotion of healthier tuck shops in schools and a range of city-wide activities on food poverty. Another consisted of a food co-op and cooking activities under the supervision of a community development worker. A third consisted of food co-ops and paid workers (not professionally trained) doing nutrition education under community dietitian supervision.
Partnerships	3	The partnerships were projects which had links with retailers. One was a community shop. Another was a food co-op. A third had been a partnership with a retailer for a community shop that had never come to fruition. Out of this experience the local community was working to establish its own shop.
Projects no longer running	2	One of these projects had come to an end but hoped to start again. The other had come to a complete end.

4 Short telephone interviews were conducted with 'non-users', i.e. people from the locale who did not use the projects.

Data analysis and presentation

Key interviews were transcribed and analysed using NUD*IST 4, a qualitative data analysis package. Preliminary notes collected from the initial telephone enquiries, notes and observations from project visits as well as summaries of other interviews were included as part of the analysis. All this material was coded and analysed thematically. The results are presented in Chapters 3 and 4. Quotations have been used in the text to illustrate key issues, and are labelled with the type of project and the interviewee (user, volunteer, or professional). A user refers to anyone who made use of what a project offered: café customers, cook & eat participants, co-op member, etc. In practice, some users become volunteers while continuing to be users. A volunteer refers to anyone who had some assigned responsibility within the project; occasionally they were paid a very small amount for expenses (e.g. £5 a week). A

professional refers to anyone with formal training and/or qualifications who was employed by a recognised body (e.g. local authority, health authority, school, health trust, church, etc.). In addition, some projects employed a worker who had no formal professional training, but was paid to do a particular job and they are referred to as a paid worker.

The self-completion questionnaires were analysed using SPSS. The characteristics of the users who attended the focus groups are summarised in Figures 1–4. The majority of our respondents were white, with less than 10 per cent from ethnic minorities. Most of the respondents were younger than 45 years and the majority had incomes of less than £7,000 per year. Figure 1 shows that the vast majority were not in paid work, although more than half had partners in work (Figure 2). Fewer than a quarter of respondents were owner occupiers (Figure 3). Figure 4 shows the reasons people gave for using their project. While more than two-thirds of those who use food projects did so for social reasons, such as to meet or make new friends, to have fun, to get out of the house, approximately a half used the food projects

Figure 1 Employment status of users who attended the focus group discussions (N = 135)

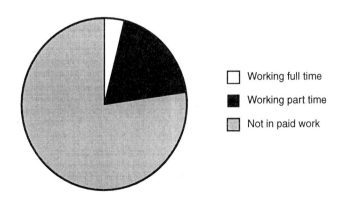

Working full time
Working part time
Not in paid work

Figure 2 Employment status of partners of users who attended the focus group discussions (N = 79)

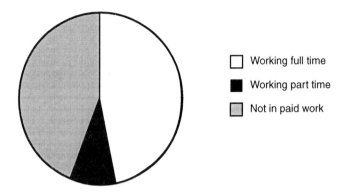

Figure 3 Housing tenure of users who attended the focus group discussions (N = 136)

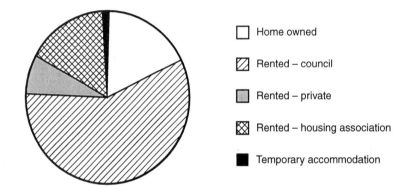

Figure 4 People's reasons for using their project (N = 79)

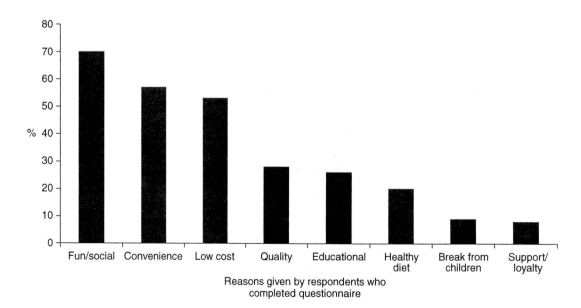

because they were convenient and sold food at low cost.

Research experience

This research was demanding for both the researchers and the projects that were involved. It soon became clear that the 'project' was much more than a single activity and it was difficult defining where the boundaries for a project lay.

Some projects seemed no more than an extension of a professional's job, but, when visited, the activity was found to have separate funding and required a different role from the professional. Sometimes the food project itself had activities that went beyond the original description, and other activities in the centre where the project was located also had an impact on nutritional outcomes but were not necessarily defined as the 'project'.

3 How food projects function

This chapter describes the processes whereby projects first come into being and subsequently function. There are many reasons why projects are set up. However, there are two main factors influencing the shape of a project: the source of the original idea, and whether or not other community-based projects exist in the area. In practice, projects fulfil a multitude of purposes for a variety of people and organisations. Disentangling these different interests is key to understanding how and why a project actually functions in a given way.

The final part of the chapter discusses project outcomes and measures of success. In Chapter 4, we go on to consider what makes projects work.

Why projects are set up

Original idea

The source of the original idea is important as it influences the type and final shape of the project. It also determines who is involved, thereby defining the skills and expertise to which the project has access.

The original idea usually came from one of three sources:

1 *A community response to a perceived local need*. For example, a community shop had been launched following loss of the local food shop.

2 *Professionals in response to the priorities and concerns of local health authorities, central government and/or institutional bodies*. The focus for these projects was the needs of low income communities and food was often only one element:

It was set up because in this area there's a very high perinatal mortality rate. There's a high rate in the city and there's an even higher rate in this area, it's something like double the national average so they decided that something should be done.
(Nutrition education: dietitian)

In some instances, professionals approached the community with predetermined agendas and strategies. In others, they spent time finding out what local people wanted to do, and used this information to implement activities or projects which helped meet their targets, while also addressing local needs. Many health professionals described this as a community development approach. For those involved in community work, the approach went beyond consultation. In either scenario, the food project was part of a wider strategy.

3 *Professionals not directly working with food and health issues*. Such professionals (community development/health workers) were often engaged in community support, e.g. community development, family support or outreach work. In these instances, food and health issues arose among a particular group and the professional supported and facilitated the development of a food initiative. Sometimes this involved engaging other relevant professionals, such as a community dietitian, especially during the initial stages of a project:

I know what it was, a lot of them wanted to lose weight, and that was one of the things they were all moaning about and I said, 'well, shall we get somebody in to talk about healthy eating?'. (Cook & eat: co-ordinator)

In the majority of projects, there had been some professional involvement in generating the original idea, either informally as a background supporter, or formally as a professional whose remit was to initiate and facilitate such projects.

Approximately one-fifth of projects had originated as an idea from a community member. In these instances a very active individual within a community had been aware of local needs and possessed relevant experience and contacts. Some had served as local councillors; others had worked as fund raisers for other local groups, or been involved in other sorts of community activities:

Um ... I was the instigator to get it going, I was an elected member at the time and was able to contact the people we needed to contact to get the funds and the start up.
(Partnership: volunteer)

Because I had started toddler groups and playgroups where I lived before, so I knew just a bit about community development, but didn't know it was called community development!
(Food co-op: volunteer)

Presence of other activities

All areas in which the projects were located were very deprived on a variety of measures (see Appendix 2). Some projects were in areas which had access to, or were receiving, regeneration funds such as Single Regeneration Budget (SRB) or City Challenge. Others were based in Health Action areas and also had access to additional resources.

The presence of existing initiatives, as well as other non-food projects, was important for two reasons. First, it meant networks for consulting the community and professionals were established and key individuals already known. New food projects could access these networks. However, sometimes previous initiatives had left a less helpful legacy, especially if they had been problematic. For example, in some projects, funding had ended and professional or community support had been abruptly withdrawn. This experience was mentioned as having left feelings of anger or apathy amongst the community. When others tried to set up a new project, they had first to overcome this resentment.

Second, other projects often served as a training ground for local people, particularly volunteers, who had gained skills, expertise and confidence. These existing projects were often a good source of local knowledge and ideas.

How projects are set up

Our understanding is that projects went through three phases in transforming an initial idea into a functioning activity (Figure 5). These phases were: accessing information; accessing professionals and/or local people; establishing the food project. These phases were not necessarily linear – indeed, they may have occurred simultaneously – but they were common to all the projects studied, regardless of the source of the original idea or individuals involved. It would be wrong to assume that the process of setting up a project was simple and straightforward. Often the opposite was true: those interviewed had experienced a complex and frustrating process, driven by many factors, the majority of which were outside their control. Some of these factors are discussed in Chapter 4 under 'Sustainability'.

Accessing information

This phase involved collecting necessary information to implement the project idea. Communities' needs were identified, information about the locale was drawn together and formalised, possible funding sources sought, and information collected about financial and other resources needed to set up a project.

All this information was required whether the individuals were professionals or community members. What differed was the emphasis placed on it and the use to which it was put. A professional might place more emphasis on accessing information about the local community: the deprivation scores for a particular area; the socio-economic profile; what other agencies and initiatives are working in an area. In contrast, community members wanted information about the practicalities of setting up and running a project, for example how to apply for funding; was a constitution necessary; how to get a project bank account; was charitable status necessary.

Oh yeah we had to run a bank account. Real formal, we had meetings and ... well, we had Health and Safety come in and checked us and then when we bought the scales, weights and measures they came in and checked the scales and things like that ... on this new one, we've actually adopted a constitution that most of the co-ops use now. (Food co-op: volunteer)

Gaining access to relevant information was often difficult for both community members and professionals. Libraries, journals and the Internet were used, as well as the knowledge and experience of (other) professionals,

Figure 5 The process of setting up a food project

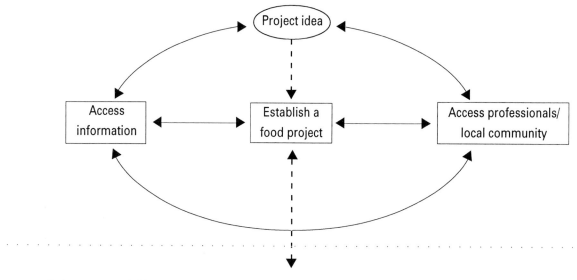

Subsequent activities

1. Involvement of other interested professionals and key community members.
2. Development of associated projects (not necessarily food related).

colleagues and (other) community members who could answer questions themselves or point in the right direction.

Different types of information are needed throughout a project's development. In most projects, information gathering was an ongoing process, as both professionals and community members sought to improve and/or continue the project. Some projects, for example, were constantly accessing information to try and secure funding:

> *We quickly exhausted the £5,000 and last year was quite a struggle to raise money from various sources. But this year ... I [found out about a] charity fund that is held by the [Health] Trust and they actually awarded us £1,500 ... on the condition that, if we get money from anywhere else, we've got to pay it back.*
> (Cook & eat: health visitor)

Others projects keen to develop new initiatives sought information about further potential activities.

Accessing professionals and/or local communities

This phase may occur both before and after the project is set up, although for the majority it was before they became operational. Whenever it occurred, this phase fulfilled one or more of three functions: consultative; a gateway; credibility.

Consultative

> *I spent quite a lot of time going round the different areas looking at what projects there already were, and who was already working there, what sort of level of activity there was ... I actually collared quite a lot of the people in the*

> *health centre and sort of ... facilitated a number of meetings with them over a year's time.*
> (Combined: health promotion worker)

The purpose of consulting professionals, often from a range of disciplines as well as the local community, was to refine the project idea; to identify key or interested local people so as to incorporate their ideas and concerns into the project; and to access funding sources. However, sometimes local community consultation was only undertaken as part of preparing funding applications. This consultative phase could generate a need for more information (see above) and the project idea could oscillate between these two phases for some considerable time.

Clearly, those consulted at both community and professional levels tended to reflect the needs and interests of particular groups, yet they could also exert considerable influence on the type and emphasis of a project. Some projects were aware of the pitfalls of a restricted consultative approach, and consulted as widely as possible. In other projects there had been very little consultation and the focus was simply that of the key professional or individual involved. For example, a dietitian, whose professional health priorities were to change eating behaviours had decided that a lack of cooking skills was the main barrier and had therefore set up cook & eat sessions. This was done without consulting local people.

The consultative phase for local people was less formal. They tended to consult like-minded individuals or their immediate social circle. For example, a key local person involved in setting up a food co-op had talked to friends, relatives and other local people with experience of co-ops.

A gateway

> *She's* [key local person] *got children, she knows what's going on locally and we can then use her expertise of that area to then perhaps do the things that we want to perhaps do. She knows all the local ... That's the thing, if you go with people who are living in the community, they know all the things that are going on locally and where's the best place to shop or where you can get the cheapest bread or where you can do this.*
> (Project no longer running: dietitian)

This phase also acted as a gateway to enable recruitment of individuals (community members or professionals) and organisations with the necessary skills, support and expertise to be involved in refining and developing the project idea. Sometimes the gateway was to further infomation: those contacted during the early stages could use their own networks to obtain more detailed or specific information. For example, community members interested in setting up a food co-op contacted health promotion workers, who used their knowledge and experience to put them in touch with other local food co-ops and national organisations.

Achieving credibility

It was important to professionals and community members that project ideas were seen to be credible, both for eliciting funding support and generating local community acceptance of project ideas. Project goals and aims had to be seen to be achievable, worthwhile and relevant, otherwise people were reluctant to get involved. An example was a food growing project which had been set up without much initial local interest. It subsequently proved very difficult to elicit

community support as the project's relevance was not apparent to local people.

This phase of 'accessing people' was often the most difficult and frustrating part of the process for all involved with trying to set up a food project. The manner and thoroughness in which professionals approached a local community, and vice versa, had affected both the type of projects chosen and how they functioned.

Professionals had often encountered difficulties trying to access local communities and establish a good working relationship with them. Trying to reconcile professional targets with community needs and expectations was at times an almost impossible task. In addition, the theory of multi-disciplinary working occasionally clashed with reality, as professionals attempted to set up projects which crossed agency boundaries:

> *I was actually in a meeting and they* [dietitians] *said 'You can't talk about food, you're not a dietitian.' So, yes, in theory, they were working in partnership with us, but to be perfectly honest, at that stage, they were more of a hindrance.*
> (Combined: health development worker)

Equally, many community members involved in setting up and running food projects had experienced difficulties in accessing professionals. In some instances, they had found it almost impossible to attract a professional's interest as often a project had not directly fitted into a specific agenda. For instance, a food partnership project had been unable to obtain the interest of health promotion workers.

In a few projects, community members were dissatisfied with the way a professional had negotiated the mutual relationship. Community members had been adamant that, if this relationship were to succeed, it had to be a two-way process. Professionals had to work with local people in projects so that those initially involved continued to feel valued and were able to retain a sense of ownership:

> One of the things that was strongest from the health promotion person's input was that she was able to feel a sense of achievement and a sense of pleasure in seeing other people achieve and recognising that she had a role in that, because she didn't own it. And I think that takes a level of maturity that not everybody can deliver in a situation like that.
> (Food co-op: health promotion worker)

Establishing a food project

The experience of those interviewed was that an original idea about a particular food project often changed, as information was collected and professionals as well as community members were consulted. Sometimes it was difficult to assess when an idea became a 'project' because of the complexity of the processes involved. In fact, for some projects, the process of change was ongoing, as they were continually evolving, either because they were adapting to meet changing needs or because they were chasing funding earmarked for specific purposes. Because of changing funding criteria, many projects had been obliged to modify their content and change their title.

All projects went through these three phases, even if not in the same order or for the same length of time.

What is needed to set up a project

Setting up a food project was often a difficult and frustrating task for all those involved. It took a considerable amount of time, energy and persistence which surprised and sometimes disappointed all concerned:

> I mean, sometimes, people offered to do things and didn't, which was very frustrating... It's hard, and sometimes I have been absolutely exasperated at meetings and said 'hang on a minute, I am not saying, you have got to go on this course'. I mean, one woman actually said, 'but you are making me feel guilty' ... right from the beginning ... the longest bit of the boring meetings was sort of agreeing a constitution, because people were saying 'Well, why do we need ...?' and really stroppy, you know, 'Why do we need a constitution? We shouldn't have to have rules and regulations.'
> (Food co-op: volunteer)

> There was a lot of anxiety from the food workers initially, because they didn't know what they were doing and that really was difficult ... from our point of view, because we weren't exactly sure either. So those first three months for them were quite a strain really. (Nutrition education: dietitian)

Three important conditions were: being realistic about time; access to skills; core support.

Time

There were two aspects to 'time', which were partly interdependent: the time needed to get the project going, and the amount of time people themselves had to give. When a professional or a community member came up with the idea of a food project, they were keen to 'get things up and running'. However, in the majority of projects this process took at least six months. The exceptions were one project that moved from the ideas stage to a fully fledged initiative in a matter of weeks, while, in contrast, in five projects this process took two or more years.

Food projects operate in very fluid environments and the length of time required to set up projects has a number of implications, especially if it becomes protracted. The circumstances and responsibilities of key individuals may change, and some may simply lose interest. Furthermore, if either a professional or a community member generates interest in a particular project, which then fails to materialise quickly, they not only risk losing credibility, but also jeopardise future support for other projects. Those who had experienced this situation had found it needed careful management so as not to lose goodwill.

It was also important for those involved in the project to have adequate time to devote to it. The majority of volunteers were very busy individuals and had other demands on their time. The requirements of the food project had to fit into their schedules. This was also true for professionals, who had to justify their involvement in a project to funders and employers:

> I mean, the big thing about the health service point of view is that I have constantly to justify to my managers why I am devoting some time to work with other organisations and what are the benefits and what are the outcomes.
> (Food provision: dietitian)

For professionals, being able to allocate sufficient time to a project depended on having adequate funding.

Access to skills

Key to setting up a food project was access to a particular combination of skills and, for the majority of food projects, this resulted in a professional person being involved. These skills included: (in general) organisation and management of resources and people; good relations with others; writing funding applications; (specific) cooking and meal management, gardening, bookkeeping. In five projects a key lay person or local community activist possessed many, although not all, of the skills required to set up the project. The effect of this was to limit professional involvement and to define the boundaries within which they operated, as key community individuals were able to do more of the tasks themselves and effectively take the place of a professional. One of the food co-ops had been set up by a lay person with experience of setting up a playgroup, and one of the partnerships relied on the skills of a retired local council worker.

Core support

In setting up food projects, it was also important to have a core group of people who could be relied upon to undertake certain tasks. Food co-ops and cafés were particularly reliant on a core group of volunteers, who were usually members of the local community. This contrasted with the cook & eat projects, which relied on interested professionals rather than volunteers.

To a degree, this core support reflected the way projects were set up. Where community development workers had been involved, they had included volunteers as a matter of course because it was part of their normal working practice. They were also able to spend time canvassing local support while setting up the project. However, the majority of projects established by health professionals had tended to use paid workers rather than rely on volunteers. Community involvement, especially during the early weeks and months, had been limited to community members who were users of the project.

Project structure and organisation

Projects had a variety of structures and organisation for overall management and day-to-day decision making. Most had some sort of management committee, which met on a regular basis and had responsibility for taking strategic decisions. Meetings were minuted and committees usually consisted of a chairperson, secretary, treasurer (or someone in control of the budget), professionals, volunteers and, when appropriate, paid workers. Those involved in running the food projects were accountable to such a committee. Only two projects had no management committee and no decision-making processes within them. Both of them were cook & eat projects; one was run by health visitors and the other by a community health worker, all of whom were accountable to a professional manager.

There were broadly two approaches to the structure and organisation of projects: 'top-down' and 'bottom-up'. At the extremes, these approaches were easily distinguishable; in a number of projects it was hard to tease out the distinct approaches. We summarise them below. There was no clear pattern that a particular type of project had a 'top-down' or 'bottom-up' approach; it was more to do with how the project itself had been set up.

The 'top-down' approach was essentially professionals making strategic decisions, deciding how and who would run the projects, with no community members on management committees. Decisions might or might not have been made after consulting local communities, but the defining feature was that responsibility for the development of the project rested with the professionals. They also largely took the day-to-day decisions in running the project, although sometimes a paid worker or volunteer would also be involved.

In contrast, the 'bottom-up' approach refers to those projects where the responsibility for developing the projects rested with local communities. This did not preclude professional involvement – indeed their role was often very important – but ownership of the idea and the responsibility for developing the project lay with the local communities. Local community members were more likely to input their ideas and shape the project, and to sit on the management committees.

'Top-down': projects managed and run by professionals

Six projects (cook & eat, food provision, nutrition education) were entirely managed by professionals (who were health visitors, dietitians, teachers, community development workers), and, where they existed, management committees had no local community representation. In one, the health worker had consulted widely in the community from the beginning; nevertheless, the project remained a professional's initiative. In another, managed and run by a community development worker, the professional had attempted to recruit volunteers to a management committee.

However, the project had been set up without much consultation with local people and the management committee failed to materialise. A third project was slightly different, in that a community dietitian had been able to draw on previous community development experience overseas to adopt a very responsive way of working with local women, although the approach was still 'top-down'. Other dietitians without that background had found working in this responsive way very difficult.

'Top-down': projects managed by professionals but run by paid workers/volunteers

Four projects (food co-op, nutrition education, partnership) were managed by professionals but were run by paid workers or volunteers. These workers had considerable flexibility and day-to-day responsibility, but their influence in shaping the overall project was limited. They essentially worked to the agenda of the professionals involved.

'Bottom-up': projects managed and run by local communities with the help of paid workers and professionals

Nine projects (café, food provision, cook & eat, combined, partnership, food co-op) whose structure and organisation were 'bottom-up' in approach, had management autonomy but often came under the aegis of a larger, umbrella organisation (a local authority, health authority or the church). A professional or paid worker (community development or outreach worker) had been recruited to help run and support the project. Their remit was to work in the community to develop initiatives addressing local needs, or to support community-led initiatives. Often, they had had greater involvement while a project was being set up.

Then, as the project developed, they had adopted a more supportive role, as volunteers took on more of the responsibility for running and managing the project.

Although there were differences in the ways in which these professionals and paid workers did their jobs, there were similarities in their approach and rationale that enabled the community to retain control of the projects. Regardless of the type of project, all these workers saw themselves as the following.

- Being there to help with some of the more difficult and onerous tasks. Sometimes this would involve sharing a task; on other occasions it was providing training or the necessary resources to do the job. This ranged from giving access to a computer for typing minutes of meetings, to helping with buying and carrying bulk orders for food co-ops:

You can't expect the volunteers to give all these hours up to run the food co-ops and also to do the sort of mundane running of the federation and pulling it together. I will prepare the minutes, I will prepare an agenda ... I will make a report back to them. (Partnership: community development worker)

- Enabling local people to direct, influence and own the food project. Paid workers also played an important role in identifying key people within a community who would help the project, and would try to bring them on board. Equally important, they would troubleshoot (making themselves aware of potential problems, particularly people – professionals or community members –

who might hinder project progress) and try to counteract adverse influences with a range of strategies.

- Occasionally acting as a 'referee' when personalities clashed.

- Helping to secure funding as and when necessary.

'Bottom-up': projects managed and run by local communities with informal support from a professional

Four projects (food co-op, café, combined) were run and managed by volunteers with background support from a professional (community health and/or development worker). Three were located in the same buildings as other community projects and the food projects were able to draw on the help, support and experience of the professionals involved there. These professionals were community/outreach workers whose remit included overseeing all the community building's activities.

What differentiated these four projects from the others was that the professional involvement was informal and unstructured. The projects did not pay these workers; project volunteers and users considered the professionals' own interest and goodwill had led to their support. While the professionals themselves confirmed this interpretation, they also pointed to their overall responsibilities to keep an eye on activities on the premises.

'Bottom-up': projects managed and run by local communities

Only two projects (food co-op, partnership) were entirely run and managed by the local communities. They were able to access advice and support from a variety of sources on their own terms (including professionals in health promotion, retailing, the Co-operative Development Agency and Small Enterprises Support Unit). What differentiated them was that responsibility for management and day-to-day running – 'ownership' – remained within the local communities, who contacted professionals as and when they deemed it appropriate. Community members acquired the necessary skills and training to enable them to undertake tasks ordinarily performed by someone with a professional background. For example, in a community shop project, volunteers received training in bookkeeping and had responsibility for doing the accounts.

Aims of the projects

Most projects had a variety of different aims and objectives. The main food aim cited was to improve eating behaviour, whether through improved food access, better cooking skills or encouragement towards healthier eating. Some projects adopted one approach, such as improving cooking skills. Other projects incorporated a number of strategies, e.g. a café provided affordable meals that were also healthier.

Only one project, a community café run by a church, had no explicit food aim. Their aim was to 'improve the physical, spiritual and educational needs of the people in the area'. The café was a means of accessing local people and providing a focal point round which they could meet:

I'm not sure if it is primarily seen as a café, I think it is seen as a place of welcome and the café is part of that welcome. (Café: vicar)

This highlights the wider aims of food projects. In fact, without exception, all the projects visited mentioned other aims: to overcome social isolation; to promote a sense of worth and well-being; to empower people; to provide training; to alleviate general health problems; and to improve the local area. Food projects were seen as helping to meet these objectives too. For instance, as in the café above, they were a route into the community, or a focus for meeting. Food projects were also seen as a way of attracting funding to achieve the wider aims. Many professionals, especially community workers, were aware that food was currently a topical issue, so they developed initiatives that would satisfy such funding requirements, while also meeting other local needs.

All those involved with the food projects were aware of the aims to do with food. Users and volunteers also stressed the importance of the social aspects and other activities, as essential to maintaining community interest and support. Different project aims were given different emphasis by individuals according to their role in the project. For example, dietitians stressed the importance of changing eating behaviour; community development and outreach workers as well as health promotion officers cited various aims, which included healthier eating, although this was usually under the guise of broader health and social aims. Volunteers and users emphasised access to food, affordable meals and social interaction. They were aware of healthier eating aims, but did not prioritise them and were sometimes cynical about them:

> *It was a PC* [politically correct] *thing at the time because they were pumping money into the estate and they thought, 'Oh, the area is a poor run down estate with a load of divs* [meaning 'stupid people'] *in there, let's give them a healthy café, some healthy eating, we'll try to teach them.'* (Café: user)

Those running projects (professionals, paid workers or volunteers) found balancing the needs of all involved very difficult; individuals often had their own agenda and reasons for being involved in the projects. Sometimes this had not mattered as projects had been able to meet these different needs, but occasionally it had proved problematic.

About half the projects had no written aims, although when asked, people could articulate them. For many, project aims were usually only formally written for funding applications. As a result projects without grant funding were less likely to have written aims and objectives. Those which had had to account to a funding body and demonstrate value for money usually had written aims and had often had to conduct some form of evaluation as well.

Funding

The main sources of funding were one-off grants from a wide variety of bodies. These included the National Lottery, City Challenge, health authorities, local authorities, Church Urban Funding, food industry-related groups such as the National Dairy Council, or various national and local charitable trusts. There were a few projects that had recourse to regular, small amounts of money to meet running costs. The money came via the organisation that employed the professional working as part of the project.

Some level of start-up funding had been

essential to all projects. The funding ranged from about £50 to initiate a small food co-op to thousands of pounds for a community shop. Sources of start-up funding were as varied as were the experiences of projects in trying to secure such money. For most, start-up funding had usually come from more than one source, unless they had specifically secured funding for the initiative. For example, funding for a café had come from the National Lottery. Some projects had obtained funding at their first attempt; others had to approach several funders before they were successful.

The amount and type of funding awarded did not appear to be related to the characteristics of an area, such as how deprived it was, but, rather, to the type of project and the individuals involved. Projects were more likely to have obtained funding if they fitted into the public health, health authority or local authority agenda, particularly if there had been involvement from a relevant professional. In these instances, there had usually been a budget to which projects could apply. Some projects had included a number of agencies and this seemed to increase the likelihood of securing funding and support.

However, while this funding had helped with start-up costs, many projects, even those involving a professional with a remit to work with a project, had still had to raise running costs. This had proved a real, and occasionally insurmountable, difficulty for many projects. For instance, a children's café had stopped running, although it had received considerable community support, because a health promotion worker had lost her funding and had been unable to continue supporting the efforts of the volunteers. Some food projects had tried to supplement or substitute for formal funding by engaging in more traditional community fund-raising efforts. These had usually been undertaken by volunteers, and had included running jumble sales, community events and writing to local businesses and charities to ask for financial support. All these *ad hoc* funding procedures had been very time-consuming and had contributed relatively little to raising the necessary funds (only £200–300).

It was not possible to calculate how much funding a particular type of food project needed. Whenever possible, funding applications were examined, but discussing them with the projects had revealed the importance of hidden subsidies, i.e. individuals and organisations providing help and support discretely and informally. These hidden sources of funding were very important to the food projects. A typical example was a food co-op, located in a community centre, which had been given free access to a minibus. This access had enabled them both to drive to the markets and obtain the food, and to distribute food orders. No money had changed hands for petrol, insurance or running costs. Instead, the food co-op had given reciprocal help as they had provided a driver as and when necessary.

User characteristics

While some food projects had targeted the whole community, others had focused attention on a specific group, such as young lone parents. Few projects were able to provide us with consistent information on users, and the following is based on information collected via the focus groups held with each project. Most of the users who attended the group discussions had been married or living as married, with two or more children. However, there were some age differences in users of the various types of projects:

- cook & eat and nutrition education project users were mainly between 15 and 34 years (apart from the project working with school children); these were the age ranges targeted by dietitians and health professionals, who tended to run such projects

- food co-ops and cafés had an older age range: 25 to 45+ years; cafés which also had luncheon clubs attracted the oldest users

- those who used food provision projects tended to be younger, between 15 and 24 years; school children used the school breakfast club

- combined food projects seeemd to appeal to those aged 35+ years.

Some cook & eat projects and cafés had specifically targeted those in need (people with social and/or eating problems). Those projects that targeted individuals sometimes found that this made recruiting difficult as people in these circumstances tend to have very difficult lives and find it hard to make regular commitments. Users themselves said they came only if they were interested in the activity, not necessarily because they thought it would help them. In addition, such targeting also meant the activity itself took a lot of energy and time to manage.

Different roles within food projects

The roles and responsibilities of individuals involved in food projects were essentially determined by the type of project. In some projects, the boundaries between professional and community member responsibilities were blurred, while in other instances they were rigidly defined. However, which actual roles any given individual fulfilled and how roles were allocated depended on the source of the original project idea. Wilcox *et al.* (1994) also found the initiator to be in a strong position to decide how much control to allow others to have, whether they be professionals or community members. In this study, the majority of the initiators had been professionals and, to a large extent, they decided how much control remained with them and how much was given to community members.

Professionals

A range of professionals were involved in the food projects. There was a general trend that:

- cook & eat and nutrition education projects involved dietitians

- food co-ops or food provision involved community development and/or health promotion officers

- community cafés involved community development workers and other community-based people such as the clergy or other church/faith group workers

- gardening projects were run by community development workers.

The flexibility which a professional was able to exercise was important both for influencing the way in which they did their job and the extent to which the local community was involved. The organisational structure and ethos of the professionals governed how they approached a local community. Health professionals (health visitors, community dietitians, health promotion workers) seemed to operate in a more rigid structure than community development or outreach workers. Some dietitians and health promotion workers had a degree of flexibility within their departments and job roles, but most had to meet fairly strict targets set by their organisation, of which local communities were probably unaware:

> Everyone at the end of the day has to justify their time, and the number of projects you have to do in a year, and you have to report back to your commissioners.
> (Food provision: health promotion worker)

Volunteers and users

Food projects had attracted users and volunteers by a variety of means. Some had been recruited through a direct approach from a professional or project user; others had heard positive reports about the project or seen information describing the activities.

Volunteers had usually helped to set up the project or had been users in the past. Some were very involved in other community activities as well as the food project. They were often well-known individuals and able to tap into local networks. In general, they did much of the practical work. A core group of volunteers was vital in sustaining and developing most projects:

> There's a lot of people who are just good old community people ... they're always the people who understand where they live, who've got quite an outgoing personality. and have got some energy to spare. (Combined : council worker)

Some food projects had only a small number of users and in food co-ops many of the volunteers were also the main users. Most projects publicised their activities within and around the local area to attract users, but direct contact and word of mouth were the most popular recruitment method, and probably the most efficient at generating loyalty. Users either knew the volunteers involved, or already used the building or centre where the project was located.

Project outcomes and measures of success

This section summarises the views of the professionals, volunteers and users on the criteria by which they judged whether or not the project worked. We have divided their views into nutritional and other outcomes because many people expect food projects to affect only food usage and nutritional intakes. However, the discussion has shown that food is only one element of project aims and activities, and non-nutritional outcomes were often regarded as equally important:

> Oh no, no, definitely not [about food only]. It's skills, it's community, it's friends, things like that. (Combined: council worker)

If the success of a food project is assessed only in nutritional terms, the project may not be judged fairly, as a large part of its work may be overlooked. In addition, when we visited projects, we often found other food-related activities going on, not formally described as part of the project, but which also had measurable food outcomes (e.g. a café that also distributed food parcels).

Measurement of outcomes must also reflect the fact that food projects are not static. They go through cycles when they are more or less successful, by whatever measures. For example, at one time a food project may have lots of users and activities, as well as considerable professional support and funding. If success was measured at this point, the project might appear in a very positive light. However, a year later, interest may have diminished because of a withdrawal of funding, or because the people involved have changed. These difficulties might take some months to resolve and the project may require help (such as professional intervention or an injection of cash) to overcome a period of relative inactivity. What is important to recognise is that a snapshot or a one-off point in time measure may not accurately reflect the success or failure of a project.

Most people, when asked whether their project worked, answered positively and were able to explain what they meant. For some, the measure was a reasonable number of regular, participating users. Other people measured success by observed changes in eating behaviour or practice, for example trying new food and/or dishes either through learning to cook them, trying them in a café, or buying ingredients through a co-op. These views were not mutually exclusive, nor held only by professionals, volunteers or users. The fact that success meant different things to different people was a challenge as there was no simple set of outcome indicators that were

straightforward to identify. For example, some dietitians defined success as improved eating behaviour; volunteers described successful projects as those that provided affordable food or access to skills, or which gave them something to do that was perceived to be of value.

Many different people referred directly to user numbers as a measure of success. In practice, user numbers varied from as few as six for a weekly cook & eat session, to 150 people per day using a café. Projects attracting low numbers often said:

- they were operating at their capacity (e.g. user numbers were dictated by kitchen size or quantity of equipment)

- they were responding to community needs, which governed project development

- their role was to work intensely with small numbers

- they were working in areas of/people with/multiple needs.

Only in one of the projects did those involved say they had failed to achieve what they had set out to do and their measure of failure was a lower uptake than planned. Indeed, the primary reason for projects or activities having failed, or struggling to survive, was lack of interest from users. The experience of most projects was that engaging local people's interest and commitment was a critical factor in 'success', and was best served by adopting a broad agenda.

Project duration was also cited by the different groups as a measure of success. Factors affecting sustainability are discussed in more detail in the next chapter.

Nutritional outcomes

Only five projects had attempted to assess changes in users' eating habits using diet diaries or food frequency questionnaires. Several projects had also used qualitative evaluations, and most people we met provided anecdotal evidence through focus groups or interviews. Most felt that, although such projects did not necessarily have a major impact on nutritional behaviour, they did have some effect. For some projects, there were obvious beneficial nutritional outcomes; for example, people received a cooked meal every day or children were fed during the summer when they had no access to school meals. There were no differences between projects run by different types of professionals and whether or not they succeeded in changing behaviour. We discuss the different types of projects and their outcomes in turn.

Users of the cook & eat sessions said they were trying the new foods and they had gained in confidence. However, trying the recipes at home depended on their having time available, and whether partners or children were willing to make changes to their diets. The projects succeeded in putting food on their agenda, even if it was only for a short period:

I think it has made me feel a bit more adventurous. I just get spurts of inspiration. (Cook & eat: user)

You feel guilty because you think, I'm not giving them that, that's rubbish food that. (Cook & eat: user)

Food co-ops usually sold cheaper fruit and vegetables. In general, users said they were regularly buying more produce. Some said they were now trying different types of fruit or vegetables as the cheaper prices made experimenting possible within a limited budget. Others said they were continuing to buy familiar foods, and, although they had not actually changed what they ate, the food was now easier to obtain:

I buy more than I would normally buy if I was going to the supermarket and then you open the fridge and think, 'Oh God, I've got that – I better cook it!' (Food co-op: user)

I'm actually trying food that I would only try in restaurants now. I got broccoli for the first time. (Food co-op: user)

It's in his sandwich box now, he always has some [fruit] *with a meal, whereas sometimes it was like, if I'd gone every day to Asda, he had two pieces of fruit a week.* (Food co-op: user)

The nutritional outcomes of food partnerships were similar to those of food co-ops.

The nutrition education projects had a variety of activities. One included cook & eat sessions run by local nutrition assistants trained by community dietitians. Their users described nutritional benefits (developing skills and trying new recipes) which were similar to those achieved by cook & eat projects run by professional dietitians. Another project worked through antenatal classes and a postnatal support group. Users had made some changes to their diets, primarily because the project made them think of how they were eating during pregnancy and how they were feeding their children:

Our kids have a lot of variety which they didn't have before. Now I cook stir fries whereas before it would have been pie and chips.
(Nutrition education: user)

[is it the project or the baby that has made you change?] *I think it's a bit of both, because if we weren't pregnant we wouldn't have got the advice and we wouldn't have changed.*
(Nutrition education: user)

One of the biggest nutritional outcomes for the dietitian involved in this project was that GPs in the surgery began prescribing folic acid to low income pregnant women. The project had clearly put nutrition on the GPs' agenda.

The nutritional outcomes of cafés depended on the food they sold. Cafés seldom tried to promote healthier diets directly, but some tried to sell healthier foods to influence people through regular eating in the café. In at least one café, there was no attempt to influence eating patterns as they simply sold good value snacks, including chips.

Combined projects had the advantage of a number of activities under an umbrella organisation or responsibility of a group. The nutritional benefits were the same as for individual activities. For example, one local authority project, which was part of a general strategy to combat health inequalities and poverty, had been able to develop new and existing relationships between organisations, and to use a range of activities. A home economist visited people at home to reach those who would not go to a group activity; a fruit and vegetable project was carried out in various

places by different volunteers, so that activities were locally specific; a healthy tuck shop in local schools gave children the opportunity to eat more healthily. This city-wide approach to food poverty had the potential of reaching greater numbers of people, yet focused on small 'locally owned' projects which were specific to small areas.

Other outcomes

All the people interviewed described social and psychological benefits which they or others had obtained. There had been no quantitative evaluation of these gains, but there had been several qualitative assessments. Volunteers, users and professionals had also gained new skills, confidence and a sense of achievement:

We're getting satisfaction because we're doing a good job. (Combined: volunteer)

It's giving these people a chance to buy and it makes them feel good because they can afford to give their kids what other folk are giving their kids so they've got a wee bit of self-respect.
(Combined: community development worker (former volunteer))

It gets people to help themselves in a way ... and I think that is what we need.
(Partnership: community development worker)

Projects had a wider impact with the local community. One food co-op became the focus for the development of a wide range of other community activities. Projects were used by key workers to generate good publicity for areas often denigrated in the local press.

The cook & eat projects were not just about learning to cook and trying new foods, positive though those experiences were. They were also about meeting other people, having crèche facilities provided and having a break from routine. People came because they looked forward to the meetings as a social event they enjoyed, and sometimes users continued to meet as a group after their course had finished:

I think the social aspect of the cooking is a major thing ... There are people there who didn't know each other before, they have started to become friends ... they are supportive of each other and feel quite comfortable with each other. They sort of share and help each other, and I know that some of them meet outside the group.
(Combined: community development worker)

I think it's a social thing ... I think it's just to socialise, because a lot of us don't get out.
(Cook & eat: user)

Cafés certainly enabled social interaction as they were a place to meet. Professionals used cafés as a way of accessing local people so as to undertake a range of community development work:

It's not just a café, it's a place where people meet, and it's a place where local people meet with each other. Also where local workers meet with local people, and it's a way of identifying local needs, just sitting and talking to somebody in a café environment.
(Café: health development worker)

The partnerships with retailers were in their infancy, but seemed to provide support, and access to training and information, and increased economic benefits. They were viewed as having a positive effect on food projects in

that they provided access to things health professionals could not provide. The actual partnerships were sometimes used to market the activity, to obtain funding and recognition.

We wanted someone to come in and look at the whole workings of all the food co-ops and kind of ... give us recommendations as to how things could be improved and moved forward ... The retailers have this idea of a 'model store' so the lady that came was keen to look at putting together ... the 'model food co-op'. So she linked with the three co-ops and spent time with them [for instance] *looking at how they organised their shelving.*
(Partnership: community development worker)

Some food projects had spin-offs that led directly to the development of other projects or activities. For example, a food-co-op had been instrumental in a local group obtaining access to a community house from the local authority. These spin-offs were also seen as good indicators of success, because the food projects were seen to have had a positive impact on the local community.

Outcome measures, nutritional or otherwise, are about measuring success. Many of the projects were sceptical that traditional outcome measures, such as changes in the consumption of fruit and vegetables, would accurately reflect projects' positive achievements. Many of the workers and volunteers were aware that 'success' was ultimately about satisfying the interests of the different groups involved. The following chapter explores how projects attempted to do this and then considers the factors which influenced sustainability.

4 Making food projects work

In this chapter, we draw out the key factors which contribute to projects being able to continue their activities (i.e. to function) in order to produce outcomes regarded as good, both by the projects themselves and in general, and therefore to project sustainability. We begin by discussing the different interests of professionals, volunteers and users by exploring their agendas, before going on to discuss the factors which contribute to the sustainability of a project.

Agendas

Wilcox and colleagues (1994) suggest that a community consists of people with a number of different interests, many of whom will have different priorities. This definition highlights the need to understand whose interests are being served by a particular food project and how any differences are reconciled. Wilcox continues that anyone involved in a community project needs a 'stake' in what happens, to sustain their interest, but that the 'stake' will be different for each individual involved. We are using the term 'agenda' to cover this idea: that is, a set of interests or specific intentions.

The Food Agenda
Food is now on the agenda of many different professionals and members of communities, including those who would not traditionally have seen food as a means of addressing social inequalities, health or environmental issues. Food currently:

> ... links all those issues. It's a cultural issue, it's a social issue ... The thing is, because food is common to everybody, you can pick whichever

bit is appropriate to any particular person. So, if somebody is coming from a health angle, you use that health angle; if somebody is coming at it from an environmental [angle], you'd use that.
> (Combined: council worker)

The actual appeal of a food project depends whether it is seen to be essentially about *food*, or about other things. The majority of projects in this study were explicit about having aims and objectives about things other than food. What was important was how these non-food aims were reconciled with those addressing nutritional issues. In practice, the different aims and objectives were used to generate and sustain interest from a diverse constituency.

Professional agenda
The professionals' agenda was largely dictated by wider directives such as *Health of the Nation* from government. These directives affected the targets imposed on professionals by their particular institution.

> There were lots of activities and money being poured into the area and professionals had to show they were doing something and a co-op was one of those projects.
> (Food co-op: community development worker)

Community development workers, for instance, were sometimes charged with increasing employment prospects by providing training and skill development. One food co-op had been set up with economic development funding with this express purpose:

> It was actually done through economic development ... it was set up with the aim of getting fruit and vegetables cheaper, I think, and healthy eating. And getting people ... not into

work, but getting people into the experience of gaining skills.
(Food co-op: community development worker)

Professionals were restricted both by the amount of time they had available and by the other agendas and targets they had to meet. Flexibility within job roles was affected by many factors, often outside the control of an individual professional. Official guidelines and agency boundaries often determined the approach used to set up and support a project. Many professionals were caught in a real dilemma. On the one hand, they had to be seen to be doing something, while, on the other, they had to justify their time and meet targets. Their experience was that community projects take time to set up and even longer before they begin to show definite outcomes. This dilemma is summed up by one dietitian:

At the beginning, it was very much allowing them to develop their ideas but obviously trying to also move the thing forward, which is always a difficulty. Working in a community development way is that you have objectives to achieve and you have obligations to meet so it's quite a hard task.
(Project no longer running: dietitian)

We described in the previous chapter the trend for different professionals to be involved in different types of food project. Professionals themselves explained their involvement in particular activities as a reflection of their professional roles, which therefore made it easier to justify their time. Dietitians were generally expected to change eating practices: cook & eat projects could be seen as part of that work. Community development or health promotion officers were often charged with improving food access: hence a food co-op. Community development workers wanted to provide local people with a place for meeting and affordable food and often cafés were seen as a means of achieving this.

Where professional involvement changed, including the withdrawal of professionals, it was more to do with being unable to meet specific targets through the project, or because of circumstances beyond their control, than as a reflection of the project's success. For example, a mobile cook & eat project had utilised dietetic services from two different healthcare trusts. One dietetic department had had to withdraw from the project because of budgetary constraints. The professionals had wanted to remain involved, but had simply not had the resources to do so. These wider issues, which may be nothing to do with projects themselves, can have major effects, pushing projects in different directions, or even causing them to stop.

We also described in the previous chapter how one type of professional may provide access to other professionals for information or expertise. Different professionals can and do work together, and expertise can be pooled to address wider health and social issues. However, if this relationship is to work, then all involved have to recognise the presence of different agendas and targets, and the need for all these to be met at some point during the project. Problems arose in food projects when different agendas and priorities were not clearly defined. This occasionally led to overlapping or clashing of professional boundaries, and several professionals would try to do the same thing, or to do quite different things, which caused tension and confusion within the projects. When professional relationships were good, the project benefited:

> I think the dietetic department had real problems with us having a dietitian within the local authority, they wanted control. That has changed now. They wanted to be involved, but they couldn't get their heads around it. I think the dietitians within the NHS are brilliant ... they are essential but we also need dietitians in the community.
> (Combined: health development worker)

Volunteer agenda

Volunteers were involved in food projects for many reasons. Some were involved because of a particular community issue such as a local shop closing:

> There's no beating about the bush, they're doing it because they see a need, and because they benefit directly in most instances. There are one or two that will do it for the greater good, but most of the time it's because there's something in it for them, whether it be that they have a store that they can access, whether it's because they've got status in the community, there's always something ... (Partnership: retail worker)

Others wanted to do something useful; some were living alone, or their children had started school and they wanted to do something worthwhile and at the same time gain companionship. For others, volunteering put some structure in their lives and gave them a sense of achievement:

> I wasn't fit enough to work and I needed something to keep my mind occupied, and in the fruit and veg business I was getting the

satisfaction that you're starting something new.
(Combined: volunteer)

Many volunteers mentioned the opportunity to help their 'community', whether that was a group of friends or the wider community such as the estate where they lived. Many mentioned the desire to 'give something back', either to society or specifically to people involved in the project who had helped them in the past:

> I offered to do a little bit more and a little bit more, and I was approached about nine to ten months ago as a community member to go on the management committee. I didn't have an inkling of what they had in store for me, but I felt quite privileged really to be able to do that. It gave me a purpose, it gave me something to think about other than what was going on in my life.
> (Café: volunteer)

It was also an opportunity to use and develop skills. Some volunteers saw this as helping them find work, as it gave them confidence and training. Others volunteered because of feelings of personal satisfaction. For many, volunteering gave them an opportunity to socialise as well as a sense of self-respect. Being a volunteer gave some sense of belonging to those who would otherwise have little focus or recognition in their lives:

> I mean, I've got women I work with just now ... that woman's secured a quarter of a million pound from the lottery ... and you get social workers coming in and attempting to tell her what to do ... She's confident enough now to say 'go away' in no uncertain terms, but it's about recognising these people and their value.
> (Partnership: community development worker)

User agenda

The reasons why people used the projects were varied, but it was usually because they obtained something they wanted and enjoyed. There were tangible outputs: cheaper fruit and vegetables; a new community activity; the opportunity to socialise and, in some instances, to gain new skills. There was also a sense of loyalty, and the desire to promote or support a community activity. Some users also went on to become project volunteers and gained further skills, etc:

> *It's because you get together, don't you? I mean, it's not just the cooking course, is it? You know, you put the world to rights while you are there!*
> (Nutrition education: user)

> *We're all sensible enough to know, yes, we're eating healthy food, but it isn't then making us go home and think, oh, we must start cooking healthy. We ate it because it was the only thing there and obviously because we liked it.*
> (Café: user)

Often, people attended the cook & eat sessions because they were free and they were social occasions that enabled them to get out of the house:

> *I thought, it'll get us out of the house and then the first week I thought – oh yes, it was brilliant and I'll come again.* (Cook & eat: user)

Those who did not use the projects did not see the need for the activity and the issues were not on their agenda. For example, cooking was seen as a mundane activity which was part of an ordinary routine; everyone did it and they did not particularly enjoy doing it, so they were not interested in finding out more. Those who were

not food co-op members said they preferred to do their own shopping, or they did not like someone else selecting their produce. The days when the co-op operated did not fit in with their benefit cycle and some could not afford to commit money even a few days in advance:

> *I think some people are scared and think, 'why are they doing this?, are they out to make money out of me?'. Not everyone trusts us.*
> (Food co-op : community development worker)

Sustainability

No single type of food project appeared to be more sustainable than another. There were many factors that affected the sustainability of food projects. Table 2 lists the ones we have identified as important and these are discussed below. Funding and community support seemed equally critical to project sustainability. Beyond that, the more facilitating factors a project exhibited, the more likely it was to thrive rather than struggle. One factor which might be thought important in sustaining projects is their structures for management and decision making. In fact, there was no consistent evidence that these had a predictable effect. Issues around ownership were much more important, as were mechanisms for reconciling different agendas and interests.

Projects appeared to go through three stages in their evolution: there was a period of *establishing* (this is where the project was getting off the ground, and accessing the appropriate information and people); a period of *consolidating* (this is when the different people involved defined their roles, territories became defined and the project either became stronger

Table 2 Factors affecting the sustainability of food projects

Facilitate	Hinder
Reconciling different agendas	Opposing agendas
Funding	Instability of funding
Community involvement	Meeting limited needs
Professional support	Lack of support
Credibility	Changing agendas
Shared ownership	Exclusively owned
Dynamic worker	
Responsiveness	

or weakened); and a third stage of *adapting* (this is when the project adapted to major change: in any agendas, location, or key personnel (professional or volunteer)). At each stage, the same factors appeared to determine whether the project was sustainable; what differs is the importance of each factor at each stage.

Projects either thrived or struggled at these different stages and there were no projects in between. When a project moved from one stage to another, there appeared to be an increased possibility of losing support from both professionals and community members. Most projects went from the establishing to the consolidating stage, but only some moved to the adapting stage. Projects which had planned a move to the adapting stage had reached a sort of 'critical mass' and, we suggest, had recourse to enough 'facilitating factors' for the transition to occur. For other projects, the change was imposed; their priorities or circumstances changed for some reason, and response was essential for survival. In some instances, 'adapting' in effect meant a new project was set up and the process began again.

Reconciling different agendas
In the first part of this chapter, we highlighted

the many different agendas which food projects have to address. Finding the common ground that enables each group to achieve what they need or want from a project often proved difficult. The key people involved needed a pragmatic approach to meeting their agendas. Aims and objectives had to be prioritised, but those involved had also to accept that not all could always be met, or acknowledged:

In terms of community development, I think what the problem tends to revolve around is that it's very difficult to actually measure what you achieve when other people are achieving it with you. If you say that [on the] principle that you've approached [it] that the community has to own the issue in the first place, and you are actually delivering. It leaves the professional looking for, well, what have I done in that? How do I measure my own success?
(Food co-op: health promotion worker)

A professional who was unable to address their own agenda immediately might not be happy with how a project was running, or where it was going, but the experience of all those involved in projects was that careful and sensitive handling was essential. Professionals spoke of the need to step back, to be diplomatic and creative, in order to maintain good relationships with the local communities while achieving targets:

You don't necessarily feel comfortable with the way everything's going and you've got to learn to express that in a way which doesn't lose your credibility, and still retains some working relationship, but, at the same time, it keeps things moving. (Food co-op: health promotion worker)

Professionals with a very strict agenda and a rigid approach to setting up a project, who could or would not show flexibility, had difficulty engaging with other professionals as well as with local people.

Sustainability was affected at every stage by the success with which projects reconciled different agendas. Projects failed to thrive at the establishing stage if they could not address the concerns of the individuals involved, and they would struggle as they moved to the consolidating phase. Projects struggled when there was discontent and people felt dissatisfied because their agenda was being ignored, particularly that of volunteers or users. Indeed, the projects that thrived through the different stages were those with volunteer and user agendas to the forefront. Projects that successfully moved from consolidating to the adapting stage, whether planned or forced by external circumstances, were those where the shift accommodated as many different agendas as possible.

Funding

Funding was one of the main factors that affected sustainability of projects. Access to funding was essential at each stage: establishing, consolidating and adapting. Where funding was short term, projects struggled to survive, as much time, effort and anxiety went into this one activity. To have funding withdrawn, or to fail in securing follow-on costs, would make demands on professionals and volunteers alike. Many projects said they had managed to obtain start-up funds, but it was finding continuation funding, or running costs, that the majority found difficult. Sometimes it proved impossible and projects had to reinvent themselves continually, so as to get any funding to carry on.

A key to projects being able to thrive was access to secure funding (or becoming self-financing). Whether or not funding was secured for a given project often depended on wider funding agendas of the institutions involved or approached, rather than the quality of the applications.

Funders also have agendas, which may or may not match those of the various interests involved in a project. Tailoring a project to meet funders' requirements, as well as reconciling different internal agendas, took time and considerable expertise. Often links or informal partnerships had to be created between those involved in a project, and other professionals or organisations, to facilitate access to funding sources. For example, a community dietitian became involved in a food co-op because local people recognised her involvement would help secure funding, while also providing them with relevant information. The dietitian also met her needs, which was to be doing something at a local level.

Maybe I'm a cynic, but I think that, yeah, it's [food] is topical at the moment. But three years down the line ...?
(Combined: community development worker)

Community involvement

> [What makes the project work?] *I think support from the local community; I think supporting structure very much from local people, because, if it's something that they need and they want and they desire, and they're involved in the practical issues, I think that you can keep it going, because some people who I'm listening to at the association are very passionate about it, they don't want it to dissolve and disappear.*
> (Café: health development worker)

For any project to be sustainable it had to have support from local people. Such support determined whether the project became established, how quickly and successfully it consolidated, and how it responded and adapted to meet changing needs. Community involvement in terms of a supply of volunteers and a critical mass of users was particularly essential for projects to move successfully to the adapting stage. All projects struggled to survive if local people showed no interest. A food growing project had difficulty generating community support, so was stuck at the establishing stage. By contrast, local volunteers were actively involved in running nearly two-thirds of the projects we visited; without their support, the projects would not have been sustainable:

> *It has a lot to do with the area and a lot of it has to do with how much community backing there was in the first place, because, in a lot of instances, what happens is that the community will say, 'yeah go for it', but you don't really have the support, you don't really have the active support and participation.*
> (Partnership: retailer)

Professional support

Professionals gave formal or informal support, depending on the project, but in all cases it was important (though not essential) for project sustainability. In certain instances, support from professionals had been instrumental in helping projects establish, consolidate and adapt. For example, a community shop which obtained access to professional support (through a community enterprise scheme) was able to set itself up more competently because of that support.

Where a project had had formal support, a professional was usually involved in the move from the establishing to the consolidating phase. However, if a professional wanted to move a project on from the consolidating to the adapting phase, they had to be particularly flexible and responsive to new ideas:

> *Yeah, it's a case of funding. I think everyone can tick over but to move up again that level you need some. I'd say they need money, of course they need money, everyone needs money, but they also need resourcing, as much as, how do you free up people who've already had those innovative ideas ... to move on to the next stage, to take it bigger than just one activity?*
> (Combined: council worker)

In one of the more successful co-ops, where key volunteers epitomised the community ownership, the co-op had been able to adapt to new community needs, moving on, enabled by diplomatic support from health promotion workers who had not tried to impose their own agenda.

Credibility

A project had to be seen as credible in terms of

ideas and activities, and in its organisation, by both professionals and the local community, otherwise they would not support it, and it would not be sustainable. Project credibility was also essential for obtaining funding.

Shared ownership

For projects to move from the establishing phase, they had to be 'owned' by more than one group or individual. Where ownership had remained exclusive, projects were less likely to respond positively to the ideas and needs of those involved. In the longer term, this had a direct impact on project sustainability. For example, projects that were owned by an individual or clique almost invariably experienced personality clashes:

> It went with everybody falling out with everybody else, and it just wasn't worth it, so we just let it go and started a new one.
> (Food co-op: community development worker)

> She [volunteer] wouldn't let anybody else … nobody could do things as good as she could do them, and whenever we tried to encourage anybody else through the doors, she would pull them down and started shouting at them.
> (Food co-op: community development worker)

Dynamic individual(s)

In most projects, one or more dynamic individual(s) had been crucial in the establishing phase, and helped the projects thrive in the other stages. These individuals were important for sustainability because they generated enthusiasm and support, which, in some instances, was even enough to compensate for the lack of other factors. Many

users and volunteers referred to the dynamic personality and commitment of the professionals involved as critical for the project. The same qualities were mentioned in relation to community members who were involved in running projects.

Projects struggled if those involved in running them were not able to maintain their own or others' interest. They also suffered if these key people fell out with each other or a particular group; or if they tried to establish exclusive ownership. Projects thrived where key energisers supported or trained new people into their roles, so that they themselves could move on – in other words, they enabled the project to be adaptive to change.

Responsiveness

Those running projects had to be responsive to changing agendas and needs of users, volunteers and professionals so as to move from one stage to another. Some projects had not progressed beyond the consolidating stage, as those running them were happy with the status quo and saw no need for change. Such projects usually had dwindling numbers of users.

Networking or building partnerships

Projects that networked to other similar projects, or that had built links with different organisations, were more likely to be sustainable. They received support, learned informally from each other and were often able to exploit other agendas for, say, funding opportunities. For instance, food co-ops in one area had linked together in a loose federation; they were individually stronger and more sustainable as a result. Other projects had formed both temporary and more formal partnerships with a retail chain or local store. Each side gained from the link: the project got business and retail training and sometimes access to cheaper supplies, and learned from the retailer experience; whilst the retailer fulfilled something on their agenda, such as staff training or community involvement.

> *The essential ingredient is to build a group of local support, so the essential ingredient is to have a policy, probably a partnership, not owned just by the Health Authority, but … a partnership created for areas of low income, which will include private businesses as well as local authorities and statutory organisations, who will commit themselves to a minimum of five years' funding, and they can decide what project, what is going to be within that, and decide what their objectives are going to be, but – they would put, say, two or three posts in there, plus some resource funding.*
> (Project no longer running: health development worker)

A number of those interviewed, particularly the professionals, valued their existing networks or partnerships. Without these networks they found themselves isolated especially when working on their own, with little support or understanding from the wider professional community. However, networking in itself did not guarantee project sustainability in the absence of the other facilitating factors described above.

Local networks tended to provide opportunities for regular, practical support tailored to local issues and needs. Volunteers, paid workers and professionals all initiated, maintained and valued these connections. The links tended to be between projects of similar types (e.g. food co-ops, community cafés) or between projects attached to common institutions (e.g. run by health visitors). By contrast, national linkages and networks were mostly used by professionals, either for specific training or to be able to contact other projects of a similar nature. In particular, the National Food Alliance/Health Education Authority food and low income database, with its details on over 120 projects, had been accessed by a number of the professionals we met, particularly those in the health sector. Those working more on community development or environmental issues had tended to access the Local Agenda 21 forum and networks, or networks for Co-operative Development.

We have outlined the key factors that were identified by respondents as contributing to making local food projects work. These views are not only those of key individuals running projects, but also of those who worked in institutions supporting the projects (such as health authorities or local authorities) or who were responsible for supervising professionals and paid workers within them.

Funding which was not piecemeal and short term, and which, most of all, was not confined to innovation and start-up, was one crucial factor in sustainability. Another was that projects need to be flexible, responsive and participative, so they can accommodate a variety of different agendas, and be owned by the local community. Food projects where these conditions were fulfilled were enthusiastically endorsed by those who used and worked in them (paid and unpaid), and seemed likely to continue thriving and adapting to local needs and expectations.

5 Conclusions and policy implications

There are many different types of food projects, found in a wide range of environments, from inner city estates to small towns and villages. They adopt a variety of approaches to management and have differing structures and organisations. Projects also differ in the degree of professional and local involvement, and they all perform a range of both food and non-food activities. However, what all the projects in this study had in common is that they work with people with low incomes, most of whom live in what are often referred to as areas of multiple needs – that is, areas which have high rates of unemployment, poor housing and other social and structural problems.

In these areas, money is often tight, food prices are higher and access to reasonably priced shops is limited. People's primary concern is to feed their family as well as their limited budget allows. Many initiatives and interventions that have tried to influence or change people's food practices have met with little success. Community-based food projects have been seen as a potential solution by professionals who have previously found working with people on low incomes difficult. Professionals have also used local food projects as a good way into a community, as a means of focusing energy and generating activities to meet community concerns. Food projects are seen as empowering local people to work in partnership with professionals in the public, voluntary and private sectors.

Given this situation, it is not surprising that there is no single formula which can guarantee the success of a food project or can prescribe which type of project works in any given situation. However, it is possible to identify good practice which helps projects work. In this chapter, we draw out what we see as the policy implications for those who would fund, set up, manage, or otherwise support food projects. The policy audience is diverse, reflecting a range of structures and settings in which food projects operate.

Ensuring sustainability

Reconciling agendas

There is a complex interaction between a number of factors which operate in local food projects, as individuals and organisations attempt to reconcile differing responsibilities, agendas and a sense of ownership. The way in which these issues are addressed affects project sustainability, because this process can either foster good working relationships between all those involved, or it can alienate individuals and organisations, leaving them reluctant to remain within a project. The role of policy should therefore be to facilitate this process by acknowledging the presence of different agendas and the importance of actively involving all those with a stake in a food project. To achieve this, national and local policies have to be flexible so as to enable agencies to be responsive to the needs of particular communities. Local community food projects work best when all those involved, professionals and local people, feel that their concerns are being addressed. Working with local communities, incorporating and drawing on their experiences and expertise, is an important element of both sustainability and success.

Funding

Secure funding is a critical factor in determining

whether a project is sustainable. Food projects with access to secure, ongoing funding spend less time and energy chasing money as secure funding leaves projects free to concentrate on meeting their aims and objectives. The finding from this study is that local food projects need access to two types of funding. First, projects need money to help them set up. However, funding to cover running costs is equally important. The experience of many projects is that it is this type of funding which is very difficult to obtain, as the guidelines of many funding bodies specifically exclude running costs. As a result, projects have constantly to change and reinvent themselves so that they qualify again for set-up funding. The cycle of transformation in which some projects are trapped is not only time-consuming but also hinders the natural development of the project.

Hidden subsidies were important to projects, both in terms of tangibles such as free access to buildings (or very reduced rents), and loan of vehicles or equipment, but also in terms of support, access to information and time given by volunteers and others. Ways to facilitate and increase such support would help food projects.

Changing professional agendas can affect the support and resources available for projects, and, as far as possible, these also need to be consistent over long periods of time. Government agendas affect the likelihood of professional support, and their ability to access funds.

Local community projects take time to set up and become established. Many projects felt that it was only as their funding was running out that they had really 'got going' and started to work well. While it is important that there should be funding available to new projects,

existing projects continue to need financial support. The challenge to the current funding system is to find a way to reward success (continue some level of funding) rather than penalise it (cease or reduce funding). In doing this, funding bodies need to be aware of the realities of community food projects so as to ensure that the outcome measures they specify and link to funding both reflect working practices and are appropriate to the settings in which projects operate.

We have documented that the impacts projects have often extend beyond nutritional outcomes to include changes in individual health and social well-being. Furthermore, although community food projects may have direct contact with only small numbers of individuals, they have the potential to influence the lives of other household members and the wider circles of friends and family. These non-food aspects of community projects are often overlooked, yet they are an integral part of them. They should be formally recognised and become part of the funding equation and be included in any evaluation.

Professionals' roles
In community food projects, professionals play a number of different roles, all of which require good working relationships with local people. In order to establish a good rapport with local communities, professionals need to have the time, resources and authority to invest in a project. Key to this is flexibility, both in the way in which they interpret their roles and in the activities they and the projects undertake.

Community-based work seldom happens quickly, or to order. Working constructively with communities so that they are viewed as part of the solution and not only as the problem takes time and trust. If professionals are to achieve these ends, they need job descriptions, realistic targets (at national and local levels) and time allocation allowances that build in the necessary flexibility of roles and increase their accessibility. Without these changes to working practices, professionals will be less able to respond to local needs and are less likely to contribute to fulfilling the aims of local food projects.

For example, some health professionals are currently working within narrowly defined structures which limit their participation in community-based activities. Often their time is constrained and highly structured, and, in practice, better suited to the demands of a clinical setting which operates an appointments system than to working in the community. The result of these contradictions between expectations and current working practices is frustration for them and for those in the community with whom they would work. If these projects are to have a beneficial impact on communities, then policies are needed that genuinely adopt and support a community development approach. A good first step would be to address such anomalies.

Many professionals also performed a further vital role, namely to help projects secure funding. Writing grant applications, finding funding sources, or supporting others to do so, were an important aspect of their involvement. This role came as a surprise to some professionals, who had had little previous relevant experience. Professionals need to be equipped with the necessary skills and knowledge base for obtaining funding, and be able to transmit such skills to others.

Time needed

A consistent finding from this research is that setting up food projects takes more time than previously thought. Most of the projects in this study had taken a couple of years to reach the consolidating phase. Short-term resourcing means that projects experience difficulties at an early stage. Policies have to reflect that time, energy and commitment are needed from all those involved (professionals and local residents) to set up and be part of a local food project. The implication for national and local policies is that there is no 'quick fix', and the aim of any policy should be to support a longer-term and more realistic approach to community food projects.

Involving communities

If local food projects are to work, then they must genuinely involve local people. The level and type of involvement has to go beyond local people as recipients, to a model in which they are active members of projects and their views and concerns are all part of the agenda. Those setting up food projects must regard local people as equal partners who have expertise and experience which are equally important to the success of the initiative.

While local food projects have great potential to meet local people's needs, they cannot be imposed from outside. There is no one project model which can be successfully parachuted into an area. This is because projects must respond and adapt to the needs and concerns of an area. The food project has to be owned by all involved, regardless of whether they are professionals or local people. Involving local communities should start at the planning stage, when decisions are being made about what type of project is required. This will ensure that local people's perceptions of their problems, their ideas for potential solutions, their knowledge about which projects will win community support will all be incorporated into the project. Involving communities and working with them are critical to determining whether a project is successful and sustainable. The implications of this for policy are once again related to the need for adequate resourcing, realistic expectations and time frames.

Food project or community initiative?

The findings from this study suggest that food projects are about more than just food. They raise awareness of, and provide means of tackling, many other issues, because food projects provide common ground on which to address problems of social isolation, confidence building, lack of skills or provision of support and advice which people would otherwise find difficult to obtain. For many professionals, they are a powerful and effective route into a community.

> It's only been in the last six months that people are saying, 'it's happening up at that community centre', and fruit and veg have been part of that. If you didn't have fruit and veg you wouldn't have the people. If you took the people away, you wouldn't have the community centre, therefore things would not be happening. They wouldn't get the funding, they wouldn't get the projects happening.
>
> (Combined: community development worker)

However, the projects also produced tangible food outcomes. In many places, the poorest have to pay high(er) prices for even basic foodstuffs because good shops are few and far between, and good quality fresh foods become unaffordable luxuries. The reality is that people have to pay bills and rent before buying fruit. Local food projects offer the chance of good food at low cost: whether ready prepared, as in food provision or cafés; raw ingredients through food co-ops or gardens, or improving skills and confidence to try new foods or dishes through cook & eat sessions. At the most basic level, food projects help address problems of physical and economic access to food.

Food is itself a powerful marker of social exclusion, both for individuals and for communities. Food projects are clearly not the only answer to addressing health inequalities, but they are important for the people they reach, and they should be part of a wider strategy to improve health and raise social capital. They require a facilitating policy environment that recognises their potential but is realistic about the problems facing those who live where food projects are found.

Measuring success

A key message to policy makers is that food projects should not be judged solely on whether they produce changes in nutrition or health outcomes measured over the long term – such as changes in blood vitamin levels, or reductions in mortality, important as these are. Rather, they should also be seen as contributing to changes in short-term nutrition indicators, such as increasing skills and confidence to use a wider range of foodstuffs than before, or to improved food purchasing or eating patterns through access to cheaper food. Measurements of process and outcomes have to become part of the definition of success.

The social gains at individual and community levels are not separate from nutritional outcomes but intrinsic to their achievement. Overcoming social isolation, giving people a sense of worth and well-being, empowering them, and raising levels of skills and training enable individuals to feel in more control of their own health and welfare. There is then the possibility to implement changes and move towards healthier eating. For these reasons food projects contribute to raising the social capital of a community.

Within this research, there were examples of individuals who started using a local community café because a friend took them along. In time, they became a volunteer cook, or served at the counter. There were instances where they received training in basic food hygiene, and simple stock-taking. People also learned skills of dealing with customers and began to take increasing day-to-day responsibility. Not only did these individuals feel better about themselves (while eating better because of low cost, good food in the café), they also received tangible and transferable skills. For a few it meant that they were able to apply for jobs for which they previously would not have had the confidence or experience.

Within the study, there were also some projects which reached people bypassed by traditional health programmes. For some individuals, some sort of involvement and even commitment to a local food project may represent an important first step towards reconstructing their lives. Any community project which works with people in vulnerable circumstances is unlikely to process large numbers. Such projects should therefore be judged in their own terms, as aiming for small but lasting changes in self-regard and personal development, of which a measurable delight in eating a wider range of (healthier) foodstuffs is one indicator.

If local food projects are to respond to community needs, they require the freedom to formulate aims that meet community priorities, especially in the short to medium term. Only then can longer-term health sector goals, of reducing diet-related morbidity and mortality, become a realistic possibility.

Policy context

Policy framework

Local food projects are only one element in the bank of policy instruments available to reduce health and social inequalities. The Green Paper *Our Healthier Nation: A Contract for Health* (Department of Health, 1998) and the Social Exclusion Unit Report (1998) *Bringing Britain Together: A National Strategy for Neighbourhood Renewal* both contain details of the range of current initiatives and possibilities. The Health Education Authority has published a number of reviews of effectiveness of different health promotion interventions with different ages, groups in need and circumstances. The most recent reviews the effectiveness of interventions to promote healthy eating in the general population (Roe *et al.*, 1997). Perhaps unsurprisingly, the review highlighted how few interventions had been aimed specifically at low income groups; of these, even fewer had been well evaluated, and of those that had, many were less effective than had been hoped. A rather different approach is to regard access to food as a statutory right, and to explore the implications for local level authorities in implementing and monitoring the achievement of this right (Killeen, 1997; Dowler, 1998).

Local food projects need to be seen in this wider context.

- Enabling people to reach shops which stock a range of healthy food commodities at a reasonable price.

- Enabling people to increase the amount of money they have to spend on food.

- Increasing the opportunity for those on low incomes to make informed choices about what they buy. Part of enabling choice is monitoring provision of clear, accessible and comprehensible information about products, and about what to choose as part of a healthy diet.

Local structures and partnerships

There is potential for creative local level partnerships, between professionals and local people. Projects can then be set up both with full local support and ownership, but also fitting into local authority or institutional agendas. This would include access to services, support, information, or funding.

In a couple of the projects, the policy of the local authority had been to co-ordinate activities on food and low income across an area. In those projects, there was evidence that this co-ordination had facilitated the development of a range of projects and activities. Nonetheless, there is a fine balance to be struck between retaining local ownership and partnership responsibilities. Some projects had resisted being part of any such structure, and some did not want to be linked to other projects. They

clearly valued their independence, and were wary of losing their identity, autonomy and ownership. They wanted to continue managing the activities in the way they wanted, without interference from outside.

In some projects, professionals, paid workers and volunteers within them felt isolated both in terms of their work and in their project aims. They felt they would benefit from being part of a wider structure, which could provide support at critical times, and access to information and skills. However, policies from the local or health authority, or from other organisations (such as churches), to encourage local project co-ordination have to be sensitive to these anxieties about loss of control, and demonstrate tangible advantages to being part of a formal structure:

Don't think that you can just do it on your own, you can't, or it is very, very difficult. Do recognise that you need to have partnership support from statutory agencies, and, if possible, from the private sector.
(Project no longer running: community health worker)

Networks

There is also potential for developing supportive local networks, whether informally between projects of the same type, or more formally through a health authority or local authority mechanism (e.g. under a regeneration scheme). We found examples of local networks operating between some projects. These were much appreciated by those we interviewed because of what they provided: encouragement and support; relevant local practical information about funding, skills training and reliable food sourcing; and advice relating to day-to-day operating procedures. Again, the challenge for the policy community is to find ways to support these local networks.

National networks, such as the National Food Alliance/Health Education Authority Food and Low Income Project Database and the National Food Alliance Food Poverty Network, are important for professionals at all levels, for paid workers and for volunteers. These organisations enable contact details as well as information about practice to be disseminated. However, despite the fact that the NFA database can be accessed by post or telephone, few of those interviewed had done this.

Documenting of process and experience is something few individual projects have been able to give time or energy to. Although many projects had been interviewed by the local press, and some workers had made brief local presentations or to conferences, more accounts are needed at national and local levels of how and why projects have been set up and what their experiences have been. People who work in projects, whether volunteers, paid workers or professionals, need support and time to provide such accounts.

Training

Capacity building

Many of the professionals, paid workers and volunteers we met during this research had had to learn different ways of working to make local food projects effective. Changes in working practices have a number of implications. First, for health professionals, for whom local food projects are a new way of working to meet health targets. Many have traditionally worked in more clinical structures, or from a therapeutic

or client perspective, and may find it difficult to start working using a community development approach. Second, those whose background is in working with communities to generate local initiatives may find operating in a food and health environment difficult. The issues are partly to do with skills, partly the framework or approach within which professionals operate, and partly appropriate technical knowledge. There are also professional boundaries, some of which are jealously guarded, both in terms of who can do what, and in terms of who can apply for what sort of funding or support. The policy implications are to provide opportunities for the exchange of information and skills, and to build understanding of how the different professions operate.

Technical needs

Access to appropriate training for all those involved is clearly one strategy to address the skills, technical knowledge and ethos of approach needed to support local food projects. Such training needs to be available for volunteers and paid workers, as well as professionals. They too can find themselves operating in new and different environments. Their training needs are different from those of professionals, but are as legitimate. Volunteers and paid workers need to develop technical skills such as bookkeeping, stock management, or catering; they need to learn management skills such as writing funding applications, chairing or servicing meetings; they also need to develop personal skills in attending and speaking at meetings, or dealing with large professional organisations. These findings are supported by the work of Russell and Scott (1997).

Professional boundaries

The career development and professional framework within which people operate has to support the innovative approaches used by those working in food projects. This is to ensure that those who spend time working with food projects (and time is a key factor) are not penalised in terms of promotion or other prospects for personal advancement. In addition, some of the barriers between professionals, in terms of territory or activities, need to be addressed. Professional boundary disputes usually occur where people/professions feel their role or status is under threat. Sometimes this perceived threat is real: a new professional group is moving into a territory, or challenging an approach. In other circumstances, such a challenge can be positive, and can move a discipline or profession on to new ways of working. Professional bodies and organisations need to acknowledge these issues and offer fostering support for those leading the way.

The most exciting prospects of local food projects are their potential to produce positive outcomes for participants and for all the workers involved: professional, paid and volunteers. Different professionals have different agendas to work to and different ways of working. Cross-disciplinary approaches can be immensely rewarding at all levels, helping to meet the various agendas and so achieve wider, more varied outcomes. Training contributes to this process, by breaking down professional compartmentalisation.

Partnerships with food retailers

A rather different form of training comes through partnership with food retailers. They can provide training, commercial and business advice and information which projects might otherwise find difficult to obtain. In their turn, local food projects can offer potential training opportunities to retailer management staff. A three-or six-month placement in a food co-op or café, in a run-down area with many social and economic problems, can be a creative challenge for a management trainee, to draw on skills and experience honed in the commercial world. Of course the same need remains, to reconcile agendas between those involved in a project and the retailers.

Volunteer support

Most local food projects depend on volunteer support. Policies such as the New Deal or Job Seeker's Allowance can affect the possibilities of involvement for potential volunteers. Changes to benefit entitlement rules can have implications for use of time and commitment: increasingly, benefit claimants have to be available for work (despite exclusion criteria). One food co-op we contacted had closed down in effect because disabled volunteers were frightened of losing their benefit entitlement:

> It was a purpose built room in the day centre and it was going like billyo and then the paper started to print ... you know, if you're doing voluntary work it would interfere with your benefit ... they came into the federation and were up front about it. Those volunteers were through, they gave us notice and everything, they finished off.
> (Partnership: community development worker)

The time and effort that volunteers are dedicating to these projects has to be appreciated in terms of work and not seen as preventing them from taking up paid employment (Knapp and Davis Smith, 1995). In fact, in some instances, food projects provide useful training.

Local food projects have great potential for improving the lives of all those who participate in them. The policy community needs to have realistic expectations, and to recognise the challenges for professionals, volunteers and local residents. The aim of policy should be to put in place structures which enable projects to become established and sustainable.

If food projects are to work, they need to have:

- flexibility
- community ownership
- patience
- committed back-up
- access to funding that is not short-term and focused only on innovation.

These are the keys to making food projects work, to the benefit of all.

References

Acheson, D. (1998) *Independent Inquiry into Inequalities in Health*. London: Department of Health

Anderson, A., Ellaway, A., Macintyre, S., McColl, K., Callander, R. and Oswald, J. (1996) *Community Food Initiatives in Scotland*. Final Report to the Health Education Board for Scotland

Benzeval, M., Judge, K. and Whitehead, M. (1995) *Tackling Inequalities in Health: An Agenda for Action*. London: King's Fund

Carstairs, V. and Morris, R. (1989) 'Deprivation and mortality: an alternative to social class?', *Community Medicine*, Vol. 11, No. 3, pp. 210–19

Department of Health (1994) *Eat Well! Action Plan from the Nutrition Task Force to Achieve the Health of the Nation Targets on Diet and Nutrition*. London: Department of Health

Department of Health (1996) *Low Income, Food, Nutrition and Health: Strategies for Improvement*. A Report from the Low Income Project Team to the Nutrition Task Force. London: Department of Health

Department of Health (1998) *Our Healthier Nation: A Contract for Health*. Green Paper, February, Cm. 3854. London: The Stationery Office

Dowler, E. (1998) 'Food as a utility: guaranteeing food security for all', *Consumer Policy Review*, Vol. 5, No. 5, pp. 162–8.

Gordon, D. and Patanzis, C. (1997) *Breadline Britain in the 1990s*. Aldershot: Ashgate Publishing Ltd

Hills, J. (1995) *Inquiry into Income and Wealth; Volume 2: A Summary of the Evidence*. York: Joseph Rowntree Foundation

James, W.P.T., Nelson, M., Ralph, A. and Leather, S. (1997) 'The contribution of nutrition to inequalities in health', *British Medical Journal*, No. 314, pp. 1545–9

Killeen, D. (1997) *Foodworks Enquiry. From Food Deserts to Food Security: An Alternative Vision*. Glasgow: The Poverty Alliance

Knapp, M. and Davis Smith, J. (1995) *The Determinants of Volunteering*. JRF Findings. Social Policy Research 75

Leather, S. (1996) *The Making of Modern Malnutrition: An Overview of Food Poverty in the UK*. London: The Caroline Walker Trust (6, Aldridge Villas, London, W11 1BP)

National Food Alliance (1994) *Food and Low Income: A Practical Guide*. London: National Food Alliance (94 White Lion Street, London N1 9PF)

National Food Alliance (1995-98) *Let Us Eat Cake!* newsletter of the Food Poverty Network. London: National Food Alliance

National Food Alliance (1998) *Food Poverty: What Are the Policy Options?* London: National Food Alliance

National Food Alliance (1999) *Making Links: A Toolkit for Local Food Projects*. London: National Food Alliance

National Food Alliance/Health Education Authority (1996) *Food and Low Income Database*. London: National Food Alliance and Health Education Authority

NUD* IST Version 4. Qualitative Solutions and Research Ltd. London: Sage Publications

Roe, L., Hunt, P., Bradshaw, H. and Rayner, M. (1997) *Health Promotion Interventions to Promote Healthy Eating in the General Population.* Health Promotion Effectiveness Reviews No. 6. London: Health Education Authority

Russell, L. and Scott, D. (1997) *The Impact of the Contract Culture on Volunteers.* JRF Findings. Social Policy Research 119

Scottish Community Diet Project (1998) *Fair Choice* newsletter of the Scottish Community Diet Project. Glasgow: Scottish Community Diet Project (c/o Scottish Consumer Council, Royal Exchange House, 100 Queen Street, Glasgow G1 3DN)

Social Exclusion Unit (1998) *Bringing Britain Together: A National Strategy for Neighbourhood Renewal.* London: The Stationery Office

The Poverty Alliance Foodworks Team (1997) *Inverclyde Food Enquiry: A Study of Food and Low Income in the Priority Partnership Area.* Glasgow: The Poverty Alliance

Wilkinson, R. (1996) *Unhealthy Societies – the Afflictions of Inequalities.* London: Routledge

Wilcox, D., Holmes, A., Kean, J., Ritchie, C. and Smith, J. (1994) *Community Participation and Empowerment: Putting Theory into Practice.* JRF Findings. Housing Summary 4

Appendix 1
Contacting the local food projects

Figure A1.1 shows the process by which all projects were contacted. It was frequently a time-consuming activity, as identifying and contacting the key person was not always straightforward. A minimum of two weeks was normally required to arrange project visits.

When a potential project had been indentified, an initial telephone call was made to the contact telephone number, to introduce the research and to collect as much information as possible about the project to ensure it was suitable for the study. Further telephone calls followed to arrange interviews and project visits. Letters and information were sent to projects explaining the purpose of the research and what would be required. Additional telephone calls were made to confirm arrangements prior to visiting the projects.

Figure A1.1 Contacting the project

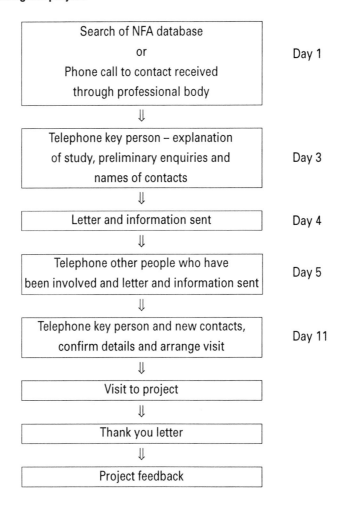

Search of NFA database or Phone call to contact received through professional body	Day 1
Telephone key person – explanation of study, preliminary enquiries and names of contacts	Day 3
Letter and information sent	Day 4
Telephone other people who have been involved and letter and information sent	Day 5
Telephone key person and new contacts, confirm details and arrange visit	Day 11
Visit to project	
Thank you letter	
Project feedback	

Appendix 2

Description of projects involved in research

Table A2.1 Cook & eat

Source of initial idea	Who runs it	Location	How it is run	Numbers of users	Length of time running	Carstairs score*
Women attending support group, which meets weekly	Initially dietitian did sessions; now run by paid worker with volunteers	Church hall	The women cook & eat once a month	20 attend weekly support sessions	1 year	3 – where course is held
Health visitors	Health visitors	Church hall	Weekly cook & eat sessions with clients who have been targeted. They attend for 6 weeks	4–5 people per session	3 years	?
A community health worker spoke to local people and to schools	Community health worker runs it weekly with the assistance of a colleague	Local community centre	Children are chosen from 2 schools; they attend weekly on 2 different days for a period of 5 weeks	8 children attend each session	2 years	4
A community development worker (CDW) and dietitian as part of coronary heart disease strategy	This is a mobile project that goes to rural villages. It involves a CDW, dietitians and a caterer	Community centres	CDW recruits users. Caterer runs the cookery; dietitians attend and give nutritional advice; women have other activities after cookery has finished, e.g. aromatherapy, first aid	6 attend weekly for 10 weeks	10 years	?

* See page 56.

A2.2 Food co-ops

Source of initial idea	Who runs it	Location	How it is run	Numbers of users	Length of time running	Carstairs score*
Health Alliance made of HA/LA/voluntary agencies/trusts. LA went through Health Alliance to start food co-op	Volunteers	Community centres with lots of different activities	2 co-ops – users have to be members. Orders placed; volunteers purchase and weigh orders. Users collect order, ready weighed, once a week	50–100 members at each co-op; 12–30 orders per week	1.5 years	5
CDW initially; stopped running so centre worker encouraged volunteers to start again	Volunteers	Community centre	Users have to be members. They place orders every week.	50 members – about 20 orders per week	5 years; then stopped; now running 7 months	5
Locality co-ordinator (background in CDW) with remit to start local projects. Local people from tenants' group attended talk on co-ops	Volunteers and CDW	Church hall	As above	43 members – approximately 20 orders per week	6 months	5
Local women who were meeting regularly	Volunteers	Community centre	As above	Over 200 members – approximately 30 orders per week	2 years from the initial idea	4
Volunteers already attending community centre and paid worker in centre	Volunteers	Community and advice centre (paid worker full time in centre)	As above	20 members – approximately 10 orders per week	1.5 years	5

Table A2.3 Food provision

Source of initial idea	Who runs it	Location	How it is run	Numbers of users	Length of time running	Carstairs score*
School nutrition action group – LA and HA to set up breakfast clubs	Schools, using volunteers?	Schools	Breakfast available daily	7 schools initially targeted; 4 stopped. Numbers vary	2 years	4
Local person started serving food from vehicle to homeless	Full-time worker (social worker) co-ordinates all the work; volunteer co-ordinator supports volunteers from different faith groups who cook and serve food	YMCA centre	Food is donated. Each volunteer group cooks once a week. Food is free to users. Donated food parcels also given to users	30 people per night	10 years	5
Environmental worker submitted grant application	Full time CDW and volunteers	Hill top above housing estate	CDW responsible for setting up and running food growing project. Volunteers help; produce distributed amongst the volunteers	Varies with season. During winter as few as 2	1 year	4

Table A2.4 Combined

Source of initial idea	Who runs it	Location	How it is run	Numbers of users	Length of time running	Carstairs score*
Local authority EHO employed full-time community nutritionist to work city-wide on food poverty	Volunteers sell fruit and vegetables; home economist visits people in their homes following referrals; school runs healthier tuck shop	Fruit and vegetables sold in community centre	Volunteers sell fruit and vegetables daily in community centre. Home economist gets referrals to visit people in their homes and gives cookery and budgeting advice which is client specific	Not known; turnover in fruit and vegetables £20–£100/ week; 55 referrals to home economist	LA working in areas for 10 years. Fruit and vegetables –1 year	5
Health promotion worker spent 1.5 years talking to local people who came up with ideas for projects. Tenants' association set up at same time.	Paid CDW oversees all projects. Cook & eat run by health visitors, home economist and CDW. Whole food co-op run by volunteers	Cook & eat in a school; co-op in centre where CDW is based	Cook & eat – users attend weekly course run by health visitors for 6 weeks; then attend course run by home economist and do hygiene certificate; have option to continue in long-term weekly course; co-op run as other co-ops	6 attend weekly for cookery	4 years	?
Health promotion generated funding to train local people; Co-op started by CDW; advice from food and health advisers	Local people trained for 10 weeks; they do cookery and other nutrition education programmes with groups or individuals in the community. Co-op run by volunteers (paid worker in centre)	Local people work in various settings including schools, drop in centres. Co-op run in community centre	Local people access local community groups and do cookery or give talks about nutrition; co-op run as other co-ops – placing orders, etc.	Local people reached 26 'hard to reach' groups; on average 257 people per month; 20 regular users at co-op	Local people work 2.5 years	4 – where co-op was situated

Table A2.5 Cafés

Source of initial idea	Who runs it	Location	How it is run	Numbers of users	Length of time running	Carstairs score*
Community health development worker and women attending cookery course; community association	Paid worker who was volunteer and volunteers who receive training	Leisure centre	Open daily for 'healthier' foods; luncheon club also run for elderly who receive cooked meal	100 per day	2 years	5
Health worker and clergy worker working with local community. Students helped assess needs in community	Volunteer runs it. Luncheon club once a week	Self-contained building which houses health worker and clergy worker. Also offer advice, homework club and other facilities in centre	Volunteer cooks for luncheon club once a week and other snacks are available at other times	8/9 regular users of luncheon club; 12–30 children use homework club	2 years	5
Church idea to set up several activities, café only one part	Volunteers cook snacks at all times of day	Self-contained building which houses paid worker who co-ordinates all work; other activities also ongoing	Snacks only available daily (used to serve cooked meals)	12–20 daily (usually same people)	10 years	5

Table A2.6 Nutrition education

Source of initial idea	Who runs it	Location	How it is run	Numbers of users	Length of time running	Carstairs score*
CDWs as part of City Challenge work; project then run by health visitor and now by dietitian and health visitor	Community dietitian and health visitors	Antenatal clinic	Dietitian attends weekly antenatal clinic; gives opportunistic nutritional advice; Bumps & Babes group run for mothers giving support and advice	250 per year at antenatal clinic	4 years	5
Dietetic department	Community food workers work independently; see dietitians weekly	Various centres, mainly in education centres	CFWs run cook & eat or other nutritional education activities in 3 targeted areas; dietitians oversee their work	36 had attended cookery session	1.5 years	?

Table A2.7 Projects which had stopped

Source of initial idea	Who runs it	Location	How it is run	Numbers of users	Length of time running	Carstairs score*
Health worker in GP surgery started cookery sessions; women attending cookery decided they wanted café	Volunteers supported informally by paid worker	Centre in area where women were living	Volunteers cooked daily during the summer for children	60/70 week	2 summers	4
Dietitian employed to address issues affecting food choice; involved local people in deciding what to do	Volunteers and dietitian	Community centre where activities carried out	Dietitian co-ordinated activities; volunteers decided what to do; included producing recipe book and weaning guide	3–4 main volunteers	1 year	?

Table A2.8 Partnerships

Source of initial idea	Who runs it	Location	How it is run	Numbers of users	Length of time running	Carstairs score*
Local person initiated it after local store closed	Local people who are paid by the profits of shop	Shop in rural town	As a business accessing produce from retailer who was there initially	250 members	10 years	4
CDW initiated co-ops; senior CDW contacted retailer for help in training local people	Food co-ops run by local people	Some co-ops in self-contained buildings; others in community centres	Person from large retail organisation attended for few months and gave advice; co-op run as above	Varies between co-ops	10 years	?

Other partnership: Local organisation campaigning for community shop, contacted large retailer and negotiations started. Retailer pulled out because of change in marketing strategy. Now local organisation facilitating local people to raise capital for, and start, local supermarket, with local recruitment of employed staff, locally sourced produce where possible. Business plan completed; raising capital and negotiating site.

Key to all tables:
CDW, community development worker; LA, local authority; HA, health authority; CFW, community food worker; EHO, environmental health worker.

* The Carstairs deprivation score is based on data from the 1991 census. It is an unweighted combination of four standardised census variables: male unemployment, car ownership, overcrowding and social class of head of household, analysed at an area level. It is a continuous variable, and the higher the score, the more deprived the area (Carstairs and Morris, 1989).

Appendix 3

Details of methods used to collect the data

Individual semi-structured interviews

Semi-structured interviews were conducted with those who were responsible for setting up and running the projects. The number of interviews carried out varied in each project as it depended on the number of people involved. In some projects, as few as four people were interviewed, and in others, ten people were interviewed. Care was taken to ensure all key people were interviewed; however, as some had moved or changed jobs, this was sometimes only possible via the telephone. The purpose of these interviews was to understand:

- how and why projects were set up

- who was involved

- the processes which lead to a 'successful'[1] and sustainable project.

The majority of interviews lasted approximately an hour-and-a-half. A total of 132 semi-structured interviews were conducted (13 on the telephone). This number of interviews was significantly higher than originally anticipated and is a finding in its own right as it reflects the high number of people who are instrumental in setting up and running the projects. Although all interviews were recorded, time and cost constraints meant that only 72 in-depth key interviews were used in the primary analysis. Other interviews were summarised by the researchers.

Focus group discussions

At least one focus group was held with users of each ongoing project.[2] In four projects, two focus groups were conducted because there were more than 30 users and, for the cook & eat sessions, some past users were asked to attend.

Between six to eight people were recruited by the project leaders, who had been asked to invite users with a range of views and experiences of the projects. This recruitment strategy was successful although, occasionally, only three to four people attended.

The aim of the focus groups was to ascertain the users' perspectives on the food projects. For example:

- what did they understand to be the aims of the project?

- did they regard the project as meeting these aims?

- did they see the project as 'successful' and what did they obtain from the project?

A total of 25 focus groups were conducted and lasted for approximately one-and-half-hours. The discussions were recorded, transcribed and analysed using NUD*IST.

Self-completion questionnaires

A self-completion questionnaire was distributed to all those who attended the focus groups. The questionnaire was tailored to each project and, as well as collecting information about project use, also gathered socio-demographic details about the respondents. Focus groups were conducted with children in one cook & eat project and the breakfast club; they were the users, but parents were asked to complete the questionnaires. Questionnaires were sent to parents with pre-paid envelopes and seven out of a possible 11 were returned.

Telephone interviews (non-users)

Short telephone interviews were conducted with people who did not use the food projects. Respondents were recruited via project workers and users who had attended the focus groups, or opportunistically when the researchers visited the food projects. The aim of these interviews was to find out why people did not use the food projects.

In some projects, it was not possible to conduct interviews with non-users because of confidentiality, difficulty contacting them and difficulty obtaining names and telephone numbers. Despite these obstacles, a total of ten interviews were conducted with non-users from seven different projects. The interviews were tape recorded (with the permission of the interviewee) and summarised by the researchers. They were then included in the analysis.

Notes

1   The meaning of successful is defined in Chapter 3.
2   It was not possible to organise focus groups in projects that had stopped, as it proved too difficult to contact past users. It was also not possible to run a focus group in one of the partnership projects.